THE BEAUTY OF

CATHERINE DOUSTEYSSIER-KHOZE is Associate Professor of French at Durham University, U.K. She is the author of numerous books, critical editions and articles on nineteenth-century literature and French cinema. Her latest book, *Claude Chabrol's Aesthetics of Opacity*, was released by Edinburgh University Press in 2018. *The Beauty of the Death Cap*, published in France in 2015, is her début novel. It won the André Dubreuil Prize awarded by the Société des Gens de Lettres and a Fondation Prince Pierre de Monaco Prize.

TINA KOVER is the translator of more than a dozen works of fiction and non-fiction, including Alexandre Dumas's *Georges*, Benoît Peeters' *Hergé: Son of Tintin*, and Négar Djavadi's *Disoriental*. Her translations have twice been nominated for the IMPAC Dublin International Literary Award and she was the recipient in 2009 of a Literary Translation Fellowship from the National Endowment for the Arts in the United States. She lives in the northeast of England. Her translation of *Who Killed the Poet?* by Luis de Miranda was previously published by Snuggly Books.

CATHERINE DOUSTEYSSIER-KHOZE

THE BEAUTY OF
THE DEATH CAP

TRANSLATED BY
TINA KOVER

THIS IS A SNUGGLY BOOK

ISBN: 978-1-943813-69-8

Originally published in French in 2015 as *La logique de l'amanite* (Editions Grasset).

THE BEAUTY OF THE DEATH CAP

In general, these fungi are of a pernicious nature, and the use of them should be altogether rejected; for if by chance they should happen to grow near a hob-nail, a piece of rusty iron, or a bit of rotten cloth, they will immediately imbibe all these foreign emanations and flavours, and transform them into poison. Who, in fact, is able to distinguish them, except those who dwell in the country, or the persons that are in the habit of gathering them? There are other circumstances, too, which render them noxious; if they grow near the hole of a serpent, for instance, or if they should happen to have been breathed upon by one when just beginning to open; being all the more disposed to imbibe the venom from their natural affinity to poisonous substances. It will therefore be as well to be on our guard during the season at which the serpents have not as yet retired to their holes for the winter. The best sign to know this by is a multitude of herbs, of trees, and of shrubs, which remain green from the time that these reptiles leave their holes till their return; indeed, the ash alone will be quite sufficient for the purpose, the leaves of it never coming out after the serpents have made their appearance, or beginning to fall before they have retired to their holes. The entire existence of the mushroom, from its birth to its death, is never more than seven days.

—PLINY THE ELDER, *The Natural History*, Book XXII.

1

For reasons that will become clear much later, I have undertaken to write a memoir, as the English say. It's the 1st of February, and I probably have a few weeks' respite left before events catch up with me. I'm writing these notes in a pink Clairefontaine notebook with grid-lined pages; highly infantilising and not my first choice, as you might imagine, but adequate for having been purchased in a bookstore and stationer's in Bourg-Lastic (a border village located between the departments of Puy-de-Dôme and Corrèze, renowned for the quality and trustworthiness of its psychiatric hospital—people check in but they never check out—and one of the last bastions of "civilization" before my final refuge, the Château de la Charlanne).

I've also managed to scavenge several pencils and a grimy white eraser (on which someone has drawn a series of little purple flowers) from the sideboard in the dining room, and with these in hand I'm ready to begin my task.

My name is Nikonor Pierre de la Charlanne. Nikonor is an old Russian name, given to me because my English mother had a Slavic bent. As a young girl she had dreamed of working as a governess in

Moscow, where she would captivate a rich, widowed prince who, enchanted by her gentleness, her accent, and the impeccable care she took of his numerous children, would waste no time in marrying her. She would spend idyllic summers in some enormous *dacha* surrounded by silver birch trees and clear, icy lakes in which the children would swim. But she was born too late, her romantic fantasies crushed by the 1917 Revolution—and, even more efficiently, by her own family's plans for her. By the early 1920s, thanks to a resolutely baroque set of circumstances I'll return to later, she found herself married to my father, a well-off gentleman farmer born and bred in Corrèze who spent his spare time studying mushrooms. My sister Anastasie and I made our appearance shortly thereafter and in concert (I've always wanted to use that expression in this context) at the Chateau de la Charlanne.

I've never known, really, if my mother blamed her family for this forced expatriation, and if she missed her native England she rarely breathed a word of it. The only hint came when, every once in a great while, she would bring out an old album filled with photographs of another time and place and containing, in a corner of the inside cover, the following gilded inscription:

Glenton Bros., Professional Photographers,
15 Main Street, Oakley Green, Berkshire, England.

For reasons I can't explain, those lines fascinated me; it was as if they contained a secret code, the vital clue to be deciphered in a treasure hunt at which only I could succeed. I even learned to pronounce the English words perfectly, with my mother's help.

One day after I had surprised her that way, sitting in the library with the album open in her lap, she agreed to tell me a little bit about some of the photos. I pressed myself into her side on the green velvet sofa, thrilled finally to have my mother all to myself, miraculously unencumbered by the presence of my clingy twin sister. Anastasie, I feel compelled to point out, was already a heavy burden on those around her even then, a full-time job that required the patience and self-sacrifice of a saint. It's very likely that my mother felt a similar sense of relief at having these precious moments alone with her beloved only son.

One photograph in particular had captured my attention in the album; the one of Auntie Lizzie, my mother's younger sister, who, to my child's eyes, bore a startling resemblance to the illustration on the cover of my copy of *Snow White and the Seven Dwarves*. She had died young of consumption, so I never had the privilege of meeting her on our rare visits to my mother's homeland. For a long time, perhaps because the photograph showed her in a huge garden enclosed by an ancient brick wall, an exquisite eighteenth-century walled garden behind which I could make out a thick forest of conifers, I believed that Auntie Lizzie *was* Snow White, and that she had perished at the hands of Uncle Banzi, whose bristling moustache and sombre gaze suggested nothing good.

Granny Ruth, with her lace mitts and ironic expression wasn't particularly reassuring either. I began to suspect the worst—that some horrendous familial intrigue must have taken place; one that could even be pieced together by leafing through the album, if you looked closely enough (which I certainly did). My poor mother suspected nothing; just continued to turn the pages, showing me with unconcealed pride the impressive estate on which she had grown up; the rose garden, the hibiscus she had loved to climb when she was my age. I thought I could make out a suspicious mound at the foot of that hibiscus; probably the rough tomb in which Auntie Lizzie's remains had been deposited by her murderers. I developed a deep loathing for England, tinged with fascination; thank goodness my mother had escaped the evil machinations of that family in time! And aside from these rare photographic episodes, as far as I could tell, she had adjusted perfectly to the bracing climate of Haute-Corrèze. I suppose the arrival of twins had hardly left her with much time to indulge in melancholy thoughts, since, as a thoroughly modern mother, she had firmly refused to leave us to a governess's care. My father, so fully a product of his generation as to be a cliché, stayed resolutely out of this kind of domestic debate—stayed out, in fact, of any discussion that might lead to any disagreement whatsoever. He was touchingly devoted to my mother, who had only one competitor for his affections, but a serious one: mycology.

My childhood was a happy one, as they say; no skeletons in the closet. No reason to linger on it, really. Besides, I share with the great Nabokov an innate aversion to any absurd Freudian interpretation—and I expect a certain amount of decorum from my readership, a bit of self-respect.

✳

In the autumn I sometimes accompanied my father on his expeditions into the forest. He would set out at the break of dawn, kitted out in wellies and an old raincoat that made him look like a Northumbrian gentleman on an inspection tour of his property—but without the requisite dog. Patchy fog rose from the Dordogne, often blanketing a large part of the fields that stretched away in front of the chateau as far as the eye could see. My father always took with him a kind of woven-reed fishing bag, into which he would deposit rare mushroom specimens he would later study with dogged patience in the chateau's stables, which he had transformed into a laboratory. Years of research had convinced him that the region produced at least three species of mushrooms unknown to mycological science. Besides being an eminent specialist on *Coprinus comatus*, the shaggy ink cap, he had written two articles which are still used as references in the field: "On the increased porosity of *Coprinus comatus* on non-calcareous soil" (written for a special issue of the journal *Etudes mycologiques* in June 1930) and "*Coprinus comatus* and *columella*: hybrids or degeneration?", published in the highly prestigious *Neomycologus* in some year I can't remember.

I probably don't need to tell you that my father's noble scientific preoccupations were of the least possible interest to me back then, or that, to his great disappointment, I never learned to distinguish the shaggy ink cap from the parasol mushroom—which, moreover, I happened to find absolutely disgusting, and referred to scathingly as *mamarotte* in the local dialect taught to me by our cook.

13

No; though I was undeniably marked by my father's mycomania, my eternal quest was for the cep, that mushroom so infinitely superior to all the more commonly-found varieties, the only one to be wholly satisfying. See the relatively decent photo I've attached here, which may capture just a tiny fraction of the mushroom's mystique. All those poets who have penned mawkish tributes to flowers, women, and birds since the classical era are vapid fools—dreadful louts, suffering from an acute atrophy of the aesthetic gland. Klimt could at least have put a cep or two in his famous birch forests, and the Russian Shishkin's unoriginal landscapes would be much more appealing today if he'd thought to brighten them up with a few boletes. I have several ideas on the subject, and if I hadn't been so thoroughly occupied by the project for which I am now wanted, rather more dead than alive, by a variety of sinister characters in a fair number of European cities, I would have written a paper entitled "The Cep in Literature and the Visual Arts: The Aesthetic(s) of Absence". Think, for example, of the single casual reference made by Mauriac during the walk taken by Thérèse Desqueyroux and Jean Azévédo; of a few hazy Nabokovian memories[1]; of a brief mention of mushrooms in Claude Chabrol's *Le Boucher*, in which the fruit of the harvest can be discerned only dimly[2]. There is surely some sort of

1 In *Speak, Memory*. Clarification provided by the author, who cherishes no illusions regarding the mycologicoliterary knowledge of his readers.
2 It is true that a few years later, Mr. Chabrol would allow the two sympathetic heroines of *La Cérémonie* (1995) to find a handful of chanterelles near a Breton hedge (highly suspect given their supposed location; they were undoubtedly linden or hazelnut girolles, which are more yellowish than orange in hue and far less

conspiracy afoot here, with a clear set of instructions: beware of the picturesque, and avoid the mushroom at all costs, unless you wish to be taken for a local storyteller or a documentarian!

My readers will undoubtedly be eager to know the circumstances under which I discovered my very first cep. It pains me to confess that the recollection of what should have been a moment of triumph, of pure joy without the slightest shadow of negativity, is in fact bittersweet—because of Anastasie. On one bright summer day, the likes of which must have featured in your own childhoods as well, I was walking with my mother and sister along a leafy path not far from the chateau, lined with oak and beech trees and, here and there, a mutinous hazel. I will not describe the location further, for preventative reasons—and, if you are even the slightest bit familiar with mycological etiquette, you will not insist.

I was three and a half years old. Already highly advanced for my age, I understood even the finer points of mushroom-hunting perfectly, thanks to an illustrated book (*Le Petit Mycologue*, 1923 edition) presented to me by my father for my second birthday. The previous autumn, he had also introduced me to what would become my white whale, my Holy Grail[1] after I had spotted it several times, though in quite an offhand, nonchalant way—in fact, he hadn't even allowed me to collect the specimens. My father clearly considered the cep to be of little importance; it was undoubtedly too common to be worthy of attention

strongly scented than the classic chanterelle).
1 I trust you will be familiar with both of these somewhat overused yet wholly appropriate literary allusions.

in his eyes. Fortunately, the paternal mycological snobbishness had had no effect on me; with the independence of spirit that is a hallmark of my character, I had already decided that the cep was *the one*. From its size to its shape to its varying hues, from the sweet little white-capped "champagne cork", or *bouchon de champagne*, to the mossy "cart-wheel" weighing up to several kilos, the cep struck me as being an extremely versatile mushroom, and therefore one unlikely to bore any person dedicating himself exclusively to its passionate pursuit. Only one thing now remained: for my mycological destiny to be sealed by a proper encounter with the cep, which I sought to hasten by all possible means, particularly an insistence from June onward that my mother take me out into the woods every day after my post-luncheon nap. But now it was already the middle of July, and the capricious bolete still evaded my grasp; a source of endless frustration. Equipped with a small wicker basket—lined with freshly-cut ferns upon which to nestle the offering that would eventually be placed there—I made my way down the path, a few meters ahead of my mother and Anastasie. It had rained heavily the night before, and the moss here resembled a beautiful green water-soaked sponge. At the exact moment I reached the old oak with the hollow trunk that marked roughly the halfway point of our route (and the first grumblings of my tiresome twin, who was inevitably hot/hungry/thirsty/had sore feet/was tired/wanted to go home), my eye was caught by a deep brown lump at the very base of the embankment.

I stopped in my tracks.

Open-mouthed and frozen, transfixed like a shrew about to be swallowed by a snake, I held my breath, wholly mesmerised by the miracle of the encounter. Even without seeing the mushroom's base, which was hidden by leaves, I was sure of my discovery. But alas, Anastasie must have seen my excitement—and before I could gather my wits, she cried out, in a voice trembling with false emotion:

"*Maman*, look over there at that mushroom! It's a cep, isn't it?"

"Yes it is, darling, well done! We'll go and pick it, and your father can tell us for sure tonight. Go on, go and pick it! We can put it in Nikonor's basket."

As the conniving little thing reached toward my first cep, I leapt on her with a deterring howl. My mother managed to separate us, but not until after I had left a well-deserved set of teeth-marks on the thief's neck. Tragically, the cep failed to survive the melee, and crumbled into perfect chestnut-and-white fragments. It had been pristine in its freshness, without even the slightest verminous infestation. I gathered the pieces of it into my basket and ran back to the chateau alone.

The affair caused an appalling fracas within the family, the details of which I will spare you. Suffice it to say that I was unjustly punished. In short, what should have been my most glorious hour was turned to ashes; and without wishing to force an allegorical significance upon the incident *a posteriori*, I will admit that I now find it quite difficult not to see in it a seed—a harbinger—of the treachery that would manifest itself in many different ways over the decades to come.

※

At the age of about twelve I discovered, quite by chance, that I possessed a rare talent for the culinary arts. In the family library, where I tended to while away my afternoons, I came upon a volume entitled *Encyclopédie culinaire du Moyen Age* (an 1886 edition with pages edged in green-gold gilt, illustrated by the proprietor of the Chat Noir cabaret himself, Rodolphe Salis) hidden beneath a dusty copy of *Le Petit Albert* (a grimoire that had been a source of endless amusement for me a few years earlier; I vividly recall concocting a hair-tonic for my sister based on dried snakeskin, one that I'll wager she hasn't forgotten either). I remained there, sprawled out on the carpet, my eyes riveted to the pages of this new discovery, for the rest of the afternoon (for an accurate mental image of this tableau, I suggest you picture young Sartre in *Les Mots*). The illustrations were particularly delightful; I can still remember one monk in a habit, depicted stirring a green sorrel soup in the most enchantingly surrealist way. The colours were vivid, violent, striking if not appetizing; ingredients with mysterious names contributed to the preparation of sauces and dishes, each more disconcerting than the last: verjus, maniquette pepper, caraway, cameline sauce, fowl with chilled sage sauce.

I was hooked.

I took notes, drew up lists, and scoured the surrounding countryside in search of roots and plants long neglected by mere mortals. My mother observed my newfound bio-culinary fervour with a mixture of anxiety and pride; had her little Nikonor, the gifted one in her brood, a veritable *enfant prodige*, found his true calling? But what would he grow up to be? A chemist? A biologist? Some sort of scientist, in any case; he would attend the École Polytechnique like great-grandfather Lucius, whose glassy-eyed portrait still occupied pride of place over the fireplace in the library . . .

I had requisitioned the kitchens (to the great displeasure of our cook Marie, who saw it as a kind of disloyal competition, a view that was not necessarily mistaken) and set up mandatory tasting sessions—not that I held my family's taste-buds in overly high esteem; my sister had had the nerve to turn her nose up at one of my specialties, a plantain salad with lardons; but I needed a regular audience, after all. I scored a dazzling triumph with my crawfish in cream sauce (the secret is to add two tablespoons of finely-ground crawfish shells; besides a slight—and desirable—thickening of the stock, this fine powder gives the sauce a beautiful yellow colour that no amount of saffron could ever equal).

My endeavours proceeded apace until the gentian soup fiasco, which would have eradicated three-quarters of the family—but after all, there is nothing resembling one root so much as another, they were forced to agree—the family physician was sworn to silence, and word of the affair never went farther than the rusty gates of the chateau. After the usual reprimand (delivered by my still-shaky parents), I was left to conduct my culinary experimentations in solitude. Even today, I cannot pass a lovage plant or a tansy leaf without a shiver of gastronomical inspiration and the remembrance of this or that long-ago, audacious combination.

Leaving aside the inconvenience of food rationing, I have no particularly unpleasant memories of the war. I spent it in the chateau's library, well-armed with nineteenth-century literature. I read the collected works of Zola (my grandfather was a fan) in 1940; Flaubert in the spring of '41; and the Goncourts (diagonally) up to the invasion of the *zone libre*—while at the same time maintaining my awareness of the era's seismological fluctuations. Vallès, Huysmans, Mirbeau, and the marvellous Robida were my companions through the Liberation; I don't believe I ever clapped eyes on a single German, which I regret, and I feel as if I missed out on a share of the action. Today's villains have nothing like the same aura or class, as we shall soon have melancholy proof. The chateau was never requisitioned, undoubtedly due to its lack of strategic importance, and yet Charlanne was still a theatre for suspicious nocturnal activity. More than once, I perceived mysterious comings and goings between the chateau and the dungeons. From the window of my bedroom in the left tower, I saw my mother and sister accompanied by thin black silhouettes; I was also witness to murmured conversations between my mother and the cook, and exchanges of covered baskets. In brief, I suspect them all of no small amount of conniving with insurrectionist elements, behind my back and my father's (the latter having adopted, since the start of the war, an affronted air he would retain until his death). He retreated into his stable-laboratory every morning at dawn, emerging only at the sound of the dinner bell.

✳

If I had to choose the decisive moment, the absolute point of no return—there always is one, even if it does not become evident until much later—I would say that it happened during a period spent in Paris in 1946, when I met Vilerne. My parents had decided that it was high time to see about my education, which had, up to then, been conducted by a series of Correzian private tutors who were well-meaning and sometimes reasonably competent, but who had all failed to instil in me the slightest sense of vocation. I had been made to understand, at the chateau, that I would not be allowed simply to sit and twiddle my thumbs until the age of thirty, and that the mycological career about which I had made vaguely interested noises (a career based solely on my father's, I must admit) would not benefit from familial support until I had obtained an adequate degree (perhaps a dissertation on the natural sciences, piped up my ever-scheming sister). In short, it was utter madness, and completely unthinkable that I would sacrifice my youthful freedom to such drivel. Swiftly marshalling my wits, I muttered that, if this was how things were to be, I would go and study law in Paris—knowing that this was the tactic of choice for dilettantes and drop-outs of every sort (allow me to refer readers to the biographies of most of the great nineteenth-century writers).

✳

So it was that, on a dreary March morning in 1946, I boarded the Paris train at the Gare de Tulle station in Corrèze. My mission was to make my way to the law faculty and introduce myself to certain professors—to "scope out the place and lay the groundwork for my future studies," as my father had put it the night before, his voice rasping slightly. He had contacted the cousin with whom I would be lodging and instructed him to report back on my actions and movements—a regrettable and completely unnecessary precaution.

I was in a disconsolate mood that day. Certainly, my departure from the chateau on the previous morning had proceeded without a hitch. Temperamentally uninclined to demonstrations of affection, I had sternly instructed my mother and sister to abstain from any ill-timed outbursts of lachrymosity. They had also been told to remain at home; it did not befit a future attorney at the Paris bar to be saddled with two tearful, rustic females; moreover, as I had explained to them, it was bad luck in Balzac. I had packed my bags in relative tranquillity, equipping myself with two classically-tailored flannel suits and the final three volumes of the Goncourt brothers' *Journal* (Charpentier et Fasquelle edition, 1887-1896). There is nothing finer to read when traveling than a journal; it is a format which lends itself admirably to the sudden stops and the jolting of wheels, the long queues at stations, the scenery and reveries that characterize any rail journey worthy of the name. And Edmond's acid-tongued prose, with its acerbic asides on Zola and its incessant complaining, has always been able to lift my spirits, and I would be in real need of a literary pick-me-up when, homesick for my native Corrèze, I was forced to plod the rainy Parisian pavements in search of my vocation.

No; the reason for my bad mood lay more in the fact that, contrary to my expectations, no one had furtively slipped me a fat envelope before my departure.

They had gone too far. Much too far.

I had been wrenched from a life of wholesome forest walks and self-guided study and thrown, without a *sou* to my name, to the wolves of the capital ("Horrible city!" in the terse words of Baudelaire). If I came to any grief, the reasons why would be clear. I consoled myself with gallows humour: *well, ha ha, at least this way they can't threaten to cut off my funds.* I didn't say a word to my father during the whole car journey, and rejected his offer of a tour of Tulle, though it is a fascinating place (it was in the heart of the old city at the close of World War One that Angèle Laval, alias *Le Corbeau* or The Poison-Pen Letter Writer of Tulle, a hysterical old maid with obsessive graphomania, wrote the missives for which she has become legendary—I had followed her activities with relish in the pages of *Le Petit Journal* several years earlier).

I can still see my father, with his frail silhouette and vague expression, giving me one last encouraging *sursum corda* before the train pulled away. Deep down, he was undoubtedly in a hurry to get back to the chateau and resume his study of the three-volume encyclopaedia of fungi that had occupied him, body and soul, since the winter. I must admit that, in those days, you couldn't expect very much else from my father; the trip to Tulle was already quite out of character. Paternal conversation at the dinner table or any other family function, if not limited to distracted and disjointed monosyllables, consisted of long dithyrambic lectures on the series of scientific watercolours commissioned in the seventeenth century by Federico Cesi, prince of Acquasparta and founder of the first scientific academy in Europe.

I can't really blame him (my father, that is). Those volumes of mycological watercolours are breathtakingly beautiful, and the history that goes along with them is hardly less interesting. I suppose I might take a moment here to enlighten you on the subject . . .

The Accademia dei Lincei, or Academy of Lynxes, was established by the Roman nobleman Federico Cesi (1585-1630). The modest ambition of its researchers was to provide a foundational array of visual data that would enable the observation, analysis, and classification of the whole of the natural world (the volumes dedicated to fungi remain the absolute peak of this ambitious taxonomic undertaking). The Lynxes had at their disposal a tool that was a precious and brand-new innovation in the early seventeenth century: the optical microscope. Like a scientific Robin Hood and his band of Merry Men, they had also resolved to correct the erroneous and tangential writings of the Ancients (Aristotle, Pliny, and Theophrastus, who had had the gall to define the aforementioned fungi as an "imperfect" plant).

Let me emphasize here the key role of one of the founding members of the Lincei, the Dutch physician and botanist Johannes Heckius (1577-1618), who had particularly caught my father's attention. Expelled from Rome by the father of his friend Cesi, who had tried to pass the very Catholic Heckius off as a covert Protestant, the latter had no choice but to undertake a long series of peripatetic wanderings across Europe, from Norway to Hungary by way of Spain, with the aim of surveying and drawing every mycological species that fell in his path. It was a highly commendable endeavour but no easy task in those days of plague, inquisition, and highway bandits. Some of his adventures, carefully recorded in a notebook, were bizarre to say the least—personally I have always wondered if he didn't overindulge in a certain type of psychotropic fungus—such as his "encounter" in north-central Europe with a mushroom "red as blood", the odor of which was so fetid that, once he had collected it, our mycologist could not remain in his saddle without ingesting, and I quote, his "anti-plague antidote". Heckius, indeed, travelled on horseback, accompanied by a single loyal servant in the purest Quixotic tradition. He ended by going stark raving mad, to the extent that he was expelled by the Accademia dei Lincei. All mycological roads, alas, do not lead to soundness of mind.

Where had my father obtained those three rare books? To the best of my knowledge, there are only two complete sets of the three volumes of *Fungi* still in existence, with the second residing in the library of the Institut de France, having been "borrowed" during the Revolution by French troops occupying Rome. I have a sneaking suspicion that one of my ancestors was among those in the city at that time, and simply made away with the other three volumes for himself—but this is only a theory, since my father never revealed the circumstances under which he had come into possession of the books.

The contribution of the Academy of Lynxes to natural history cannot be overestimated. In the three volumes dedicated to fungi, every species of mushroom in Umbria is examined under a microscope, inventoried, depicted in watercolour, and accompanied by a description of the various stages of its maturation, as well as detailed technical information on the colour, odour, taste, weight, and provenance of the specimen. In brief, these books are both scientific tomes and works of art unsurpassed in refinement and meticulousness, for which I confess my admiration, like my progenitor's, is boundless. You will not be surprised, therefore, to learn that after the latter's death "from natural causes", the volumes in question passed into my possession.

2

During one of my rare visits to the château—it must have been in the early fifties—I found my father in a state of feverish agitation. He had summoned me to his laboratory immediately after dinner and was now pacing in long strides, shoes thumping on the three-hundred-year-old oak parquet floor. His rage, it turned out, was directed at the unfortunate Claude-Casimir Gillet, author of an eminent tome entitled *Les Champignons qui croissent en France: description et iconographie, propriétés utile ou vénéneuses* (1878).[1]

"That addle-brained cretin!" he sputtered furiously, "You have no idea—he's misinformed three generations of mycologists—the entire classification of hymenomycetes will have to be redone . . ."

A lengthy diatribe followed, of which I understood only a few snippets. The problem, it seemed, had to do with Gillet's placement of the death cap within the Agaricaceae family. My father took issue with the author's assertion that the *Amanita*'s volva leaves visible traces as the specimen grows. I was tempted to point out that Brongniart's *Essai de classification naturelle des*

---

1 *Mushrooms that grow in France: description and iconography; useful or poisonous attributes.*

27

champignons had made the same taxonomical claim in 1825, and thus it was unfair to saddle Claude-Casimir with all of the blame—but my father, without paying the slightest attention to me, launched into a disjointed tangent on rates of harmlessness, which in the *Amanita* are inversely proportional to the retention of the collar.

Abruptly he stopped pacing with a great wooden creak, his ice-blue gaze pinning me where I stood.

"If you think I don't know what you're getting up to in Paris, my boy, you're very much mistaken. I haven't said anything to your mother; she still thinks you're enrolled at the Sorbonne, and was so thrilled by the "special mention" made of the "young law student of the year by Professor Laborie" that I didn't have the heart to set her straight. Did you think you could fool me? My feelers are everywhere; you had better shape up, and fast. I order you to put an end to the odious trafficking in which you have involved yourself, dishonouring our family name! If you don't, I will be forced to come to Paris myself and take the most draconian of measures, do you understand me? I have already contacted Monsieur Desnos[1] and am meeting with him next week to review certain parts of my will."

I remained outwardly impassive. I couldn't have been more shaken if he had forced me to swallow the powdered volva of the *Amanita phalloides*, but I refused to let my feelings show. It is this strength of character, this infallible coolness in the face of adversity, that has enabled me to extricate myself from the most hopeless situations, and brought me to where I am today.

---

1 Our family attorney.

I murmured something about a misunderstanding, a mistake that would soon be cleared up, and rapidly took my leave. My father seemed to have lost all interest in the conversation, and when I shut the door behind me he was bent over a microscope, surrounded by books and glass slides, the very image of a mad scientist, absent-minded and perfectly harmless (think Professor Calculus in *Tintin*). Had I suffered some sort of auditory hallucination? I ruminated on it for the rest of the evening. My sister must have stuck her nose into it, the snooping little harpy; she was undoubtedly sick with obsessive jealousy of me! I mulled over the various recourses open to me. I had to find a solution that would lead to a satisfying conclusion for all parties concerned.

Sleep eluded me that night. I'd like to think that the duellist awaiting the dawn before a potentially fatal confrontation experiences a similar state of mind.

✳

It came to me at sunrise, as delicate rays of light played on the wall of my bedroom.

Nicander would have the solution I sought.

I have always had a weakness for Nicander of Colophon (b. 197 B.C.), perhaps because his name isn't so very different from my own, and because I sense that, beyond our sonorous similarities, we share certain elective affinities based on long years of scholarship that have only been strengthened by the passage of centuries. A simple Internet search will tell you that Nicander was a Greek physician, poet, and grammarian. So far, so good—though in my humble opinion, his writings on grammar, literature, and mythology cannot hold a candle to his *Alexipharmaca*, a 630-hexameter poem on poisons and their antidotes. Indeed, it is when we come to his masterpiece, *Alexipharmaca*, that things begin to take a wrong turn. A certain online encyclopaedia which I cannot bring myself to name states that "these writings contain a large number of errors and superstitions"; without wishing to seem like a grumpy, reactionary old man (I am irreproachably modern, and my adoration of the Internet knows no bounds, not least for the invaluable logistical support it provides to a man in my line of work), I would dearly love to get my hands on the rapscallion who felt obliged to bequeath these absurdities to posterity. *Alexipharmaca*, despite its poetic form, is, in fact, a model of scientific rigour, and a medical text whose authority still stands even after two millennia.

Preceded by *Theriaca*, a treatise on the wounds inflicted by snakes, scorpions, and other venomous creatures, *Alexipharmaca* is, for its part, dedicated to poisons absorbed orally—rather than cutaneously, as in *Theriaca*. In the text, Nicander identifies twenty-one poisons of animal, vegetal, or mineral origin, describes the individual characteristics of each type of toxicity, and suggests antidotal treatments. The tripartite structure of the poem is admirable in its clarity; a physical description of the solution into which the poison is mixed is followed by a recitation of the clinical symptoms that follow its ingestion, and then by a list of specific treatments.

I lingered over the first two parts of each section in particular.

The *Alexipharmaca*, uniquely in Nicander's prolific output, is accompanied by forty-one miniature illustrations, remarkably fine in their execution, which guide the reader through his journey and provide an agreeable counterpoint to the aridity of the scientific material. The entwined serpents are particularly captivating; Nicander's imagery is reminiscent in many ways of the nightmarish visions of Bosch, and its evocative power far surpasses that of the somewhat flat colour plates found in Buffon's *Histoire Naturelle*.

※

The funeral took place a week later, in the cemetery of the Château de la Charlanne. My father had fallen suddenly ill just after my departure for Paris, and died without regaining consciousness after two full days of agony. Grivaud, our family physician, with the confidence (and incompetence) that were his stock in trade, had blamed the death on acute pancreatitis and signed the death certificate without hesitation. I had been notified by telegram, and decided to return home for the occasion even though the timing was quite inconvenient for me professionally.

The ceremony was sparsely attended; besides my mother and sister there were some fellow residents of the neighbourhood, but so few that, despite their habitual fondness for this type of surprise party, they could be counted on one hand. My father, it must be admitted, had not been the most popular man in the area; he had forbidden all access to his lands, and was never slow in bringing out his shotgun when a hunter or mushroom-gatherer (peace be upon them) strayed onto the property.

Father Sandeyron murmured a passage from the Gospels in a monotone. It was, if memory serves, a fairly obscure parable from Mark about the seed that grew all by itself. I failed to see even the slightest connection to my father's life in it; logical thinking was never the good priest's strong suit. I soon grew bored, and transferred my interest to the tall, rather attractive young man standing beside my sister. Was there something afoot? I had not seen him at the château; he must only just have arrived. All sorts of things were hidden from me in this family. I would obviously have to keep an eye on the situation. And old Legrandin, whose property adjoined our own, kept darting sideways glances at me, which I found most displeasing.

The open-air service seemed to last forever.

Restless, I allowed my gaze to drift over the pines surrounding the little weed-choked cemetery. Once, on a bright autumn morning, I had found three large red ceps nestled together among those trees. I love this peaceful place, so mossy and nostalgic; so little marked by traces of the present. Several generations of my father's family are buried here; on the oldest headstone can barely be discerned the name of Jehan de la C. and the dates 1546 (or 1548) and 1577. Alongside him, lying beneath this ground where the mineral and the vegetal mingle in almost Angkorian tones, are a multitude of Françoises and Charleses, one Valérien, and two Aristides (I will undoubtedly have occasion to return here). As a child, the family cemetery served as a refuge during my attempts to escape the lessons of my imbecilic tutors, or some idiotic scheme of my sister's. I would settle myself comfortably, bread and jam (preferably rhubarb) in hand, against Jehan de la C.'s tombstone and daydream to my heart's content while contemplating the pines, twisted against the sky. It was undoubtedly there, *à ce moment exact*, that I gained my profound sense of family, and of the importance of lineage. Even now, when I leave the château by the rear entrance—the one adjoining the *oubliettes*—I find myself drawn along the little hazel-bordered path to the old cemetery, passing through this into the forest of pines, which, as I walk, give way to majestic beeches and small, gnarled oaks. After a good ten minutes of walking I reach a pond, its waters green and calm, stocked with greyish Hiroshige carp. The road, a private one, leads to the Dordogne river—but if you leave it to roam through these woods and deep, unexpected gorges, you can go for several kilometres without encountering another living soul. These wanderings have always been able to bring me a certain degree of peace, no matter how great my initial state of agitation.

On that day, however, my walk was a short one. Seeking to avoid the well-worn formalities, I slipped away as soon as the burial was over and followed the Dordogne road for a few hundred metres. It was late autumn. Dry leaves and branches cracked beneath my feet, and a sharp, cold wind drove me onward. The wild, bleak landscape mirrored my own dismal mood. Obeying a sort of automatic impulse from somewhere in the deepest part of myself, my eyes scanned the underbrush, looking for mushrooms (I have never been able to walk in a wood, even in the depths of winter, without searching the forest floor for a hypothetical cep). Every forest, every tree in this place has its own history for me, from a legendary harvest of thirty or forty ceps together, to a fairy ring of girolles several kilos in weight, discovered on a mossy mound.

I was unsettled. I had a kind of gut feeling that I was not in possession of all the information; there was something I didn't know, something that, if I wasn't very careful, might prove fatal. And yet, I had taken every precaution, and I grew calmer as I went over the sequence in my mind. I knew that certain facts, scattered across time and space, had the potential—if someone thought to fit them together, and if viewed from a certain angle—to draw unwelcome attention, or even to lead to a damning interpretation. But these facts could only be accessed all together by a very small number of persons, namely my mother and my sister, whose lack of perspicacity required no further proof.[1] Now, despite everything, it was time to return to the château, to see how things were panning out. As I turned, I only just avoided tripping over a green brittlegill mushroom (*Russula virescens*) growing mischievously in the middle of the path.

I realised the seriousness of the situation as soon as I opened the door of the drawing room: my mother had brought out great-aunt Hermione's liqueur glasses. Dramatically attired in a black velvet dress, she greeted me with affected exasperation.

---

1 Alas, it is never a good idea to underestimate weak people and idiots, as I was to learn later, in other circumstances, and I bear an extremely unsightly scar on my abdomen as a painful reminder of my mistake. To quote the great Japanese thinker Sakurazawa Taeka, who is unfairly forgotten today: "Even the humble edamame shell can become a splinter in the heel of the Buddha"

34

"At last, Nikonor; how on earth could you disappear like that! And on today, of all days! Everyone was wondering what had happened to you; I even sent Antonin and Anastasie out to look in your poor father's laboratory!—[strangled sob]—Antonin, this is my son, Nikonor. Don't mind him too much, please; he was terribly attached to his papa, whose passion for biology he shares." (My mother had always been faintly embarrassed by our mycological interests, which she considered parochial and *nerdy*, much preferring the major all-embracing scientific disciplines.) "Nikonor is a brilliant law student, Antonin. He is the pillar of our family, and our great hope.

"Nikonor, this is Antonin Berg, who has had the great kindness to come and support Anastasie in the midst of our suffering. You will have a bit of elderberry liqueur, Antonin, I hope? It's a specialty of the region." My mother continued to pontificate in this vein for an eternity, throwing ghastly simpering little smiles at the aforementioned Antonin from time to time. The shamelessness! She had only just buried her husband, her life's companion, and she was already scheming to fob her daughter off on a suitor! And one, moreover, who had not been approved by the head of the family!

I returned Antonin's greeting and seated myself nonchalantly on the settee in the *cantou*[1]. Berg . . . *Berg* . . . the name sounded vaguely familiar to me. Even as I asked a series of polite yet pointed questions about his education and his family—his father had founded a large agronomical company near Ussel; I had seen the

---

1 A recessed alcove with benches surrounding a fireplace, typical of many homes here in the centre of France.

name on the sacks of fertilizer old Legrandin ordered by the truckload—I devoted myself to a surreptitious examination of the younger Berg. How on earth had the scatterbrained Anastasie, sent to school at the convent in Ussel for an education befitting the daughter of a prominent family, managed to get her hooks into such a man? Ironically, Antonin looked a great deal like me (most mortals would be in agreement on this point: we were both tall and strongly built, with chestnut hair and penetrating blue eyes; there were a number of objective and quantifiable criteria present), but only in the way a caricature resembles the original—for even though he was of indisputable physical beauty, he lacked even the slightest trace of refinement, of nobility of feature, and he would not have been out of place in the disreputable spots I sometimes frequented in the course of my professional activities. In any case, the resemblance could not possibly have been lost on Anastasie, the perverted little slut. What was she playing at? I thought I could detect the hint of a mocking little smile on Antonin's lips. I carefully avoided Anastasie's gleeful gaze. I had known forever that the ultimate goal of her existence, the sole desire of her whole slender being, was to hurt me, to destroy me, to annihilate me—and Antonin was indeed a dazzling addition to her arsenal; a resounding success, a triumph of provocation and sisterly pettiness.

Like a proper potential brother-in-law, I offered to give Antonin a tour of the property. We had just finished a rather successful country-style dinner of roasted pheasant, chestnuts *au jus*, and oven-baked endives (I had refused the dessert of apple tart; the worthy Marie, though one of the most highly-reputed *cuisinières* in the county, had never been able to give her pastry the lightness and delicacy it required), with which Antonin had stuffed himself most unattractively, devouring third helpings of everything and not holding back when it came to the Bordeaux brought up from my father's wine cellar, either. Anastasie herself even seemed a touch put out, if one might attribute even the slightest sense of decency to such a person, fiddling nervously with the mother-of-pearl buttons of her blouse and not daring to look at me.

I took Antonin into the library to begin the tour, but he showed little interest in the maps, old books, and rare manuscripts displayed there. I'm afraid I wasted my time lecturing him on the marvellous futuristic inventions of Robida (at the risk of arousing envy, I will tell you that I possess first editions of *Le Vingtième siècle* [1883], *La Guerre au vingtième siècle* [1887], and *La Vie électrique* [1890]). Any conservator or collector worth his salt (to use the charming English expression, so much more distinguished than the peanut-based French equivalent, *valoir son pesant de cacahuètes*) would gladly have killed his own mother and father to be in Antonin's place, but the boy merely looked at the wood panelling and the oil portrait of great-grandfather Lucius, and nodded complacently.

He seemed to me to be of an extremely limited intellect.

It is in intermingling with this sort of flawed, dull-witted stock that we bring about the degeneration of our race, as masterfully demonstrated by Bénédict Augustin Morel (the Freud of France) in a book that should have occupied a place on one of these shelves. Reading it would certainly have been of great benefit to Anastasie—and many others, as it happens. Sighing inwardly, I suggested that we next pay a visit to the keep, with its hundred and eleven steps and its breathtaking view of the Dordogne. Antonin Berg followed me without any particular enthusiasm; undoubtedly out of sheer courteous fatigue, and also because no better option had been offered to him. As he had indulged a bit too generously in the paternal Bordeaux, his steps were not quite straight, and he began swaying even as we ascended the first few steps. I had to help steady him more than once.

There can be no question that this tipsiness acted as a catalyst to his fall.

His death was instantaneous, contrary to what those overzealous hack journalists wrote afterward.

✳

This was indeed quite a lot of tragedy to befall the peaceful hamlet of Charlanne; a veritable massacre, in fact, if one insisted on calculating the statistics in terms of the number of deaths per square meter in the span of less than one week (that old busybody Legrandin didn't provide a generous luncheon to the carp in our fishpond until the following spring, so there was no need to add him to the tally). In short, it seemed that a curse had fallen upon our family and those close to us. We made headlines in all the local papers for at least a hundred kilometres in every direction. *La Vie corrézienne* even managed to procure a somewhat blurry photo of the château, which to the best of my knowledge isn't visible from the main road; the photographer must have broken every rule in the book about respecting private property, which would have greatly displeased my poor father, *requiescat in pace*:

Misfortune strikes the residents of the Château de la Charlanne anew. On the very day of the burial of Pierre de la Charlanne, eminent mycologist and much-lamented expert on the shaggy ink cap, young Antonin Berg, son of Paul Berg of the Berg-Agronomie company in Ussel, met his death via a 30-metre fall from the right-hand tower of the keep. Despite the exhaustive efforts of the castle's young owner, Nikonor de la Charlanne, to revive him, Antonin never regained consciousness. As a friend of the family, Antonin had attended the funeral in order to provide moral support to the widow of Pierre de la Charlanne and to her two children, Anastasie and Nikonor. According to our sources, Antonin was on the point of requesting the hand of Mademoiselle Anastasie Hélène de la Charlanne in marriage. The young man, who became slightly unwell after a too-rapid ascension of a more than 100-step spiral staircase, probably wished to get a breath of air and may have leaned imprudently out the window of the keep, subsequently losing his balance. His friend Nikonor de la Charlanne, who had just reached the top of the tower, could only watch helplessly as he fell. Rushing down to the courtyard of the château, Nikonor tried in vain to aid his unfortunate friend, but alas, it was too late. This unthinkable tragedy has put a premature end to a young life poised on the brink of great accomplishment . . .

La Gazette de Champagnac also chimed in breathlessly:

> *Fatal Fall from the Tower: Two Deaths in Three Days at La Charlanne. What is it about certain places that seem marked for affliction? In less than three days, death has knocked twice on the doors of the Château de la Charlanne, idyllic ancestral home of the Sanderres de la Charlanne, overlooking the rugged gorges of the Dordogne . . .*

For its part, *L'Echo chrétien de Bort-les-Orgues* noted helpfully that "the Château de la Charlanne seems to have been abandoned, during these three terrible days, by the fireflies of hope". Speaking of fireflies, I must tell you here that those fragile little fairies of the summer's eve have all but vanished from la Charlanne over the past ten or twenty years, an ecological disaster which has caused me no end of worry. I suspect the descendants of old Legrandin, who, having passed the management of the farm next to ours from generation to generation, have tended to use pesticides that are particularly harmful to fireflies. It is on my list. If God spares me, I swear I will investigate one of these days. As an ardent defender of the environment and a champion of sustainable development, I am appalled by any damage to the ecosystem caused by this sort of polluting human activity. One must know, sometimes, when to invest one's energies in a good cause, and I have certainly never been the type to shy away from a difficult situation . . .

✳

As the country air was beginning to become insalubrious for me, I departed as quickly as possible for Paris, without waiting to attend the wake honouring the Berg company's heir. Anyway, mushroom season was over, and winter was approaching in leaps and bounds. Always a sharp-eyed observer of omens, I had already drawn all sorts of irrefutably dark conclusions from the mournful honks of a flock of wild geese seen flying over the château. Besides, "urgent business" required my attention back in the capital.

3

Today, with a poignant mixture of trepidation and nostalgia, I have decided to take a trip down memory lane, during which I will pause here and there to linger over a particular recollection, to turn it over and over in my hands, like a pretty white pebble gathered in a stream, in order to see if something rises to the surface of my mind that might otherwise have escaped me. It happens sometimes that these white pebbles are really snowballs, triggering a massive avalanche of flash-backs which are not altogether pleasant. I have spent many days and nights now suspended in a bubble of hermeneutic delirium, trying to thread the impossibly narrow eye of a needle—that is, to tease the meaning out of a jagged shard of my past. And I have been forced to admit to an unavoidable conclusion: that not everything can be explained. We must learn to resign ourselves to the opacity, the mystery, that surrounds parts of certain events, certain destinies.

There is nothing edible remaining in the pantry. Since I cherish no particular hopes with regard to the quality of provisions offered by the closest village "grocery" (which is, in fact, a vulgar "mini-mart", utterly common in its mediocrity, if not its exorbitant prices. A word to tourists steeped in clichés concerning the charms of the French countryside: butcher shop, *boulangerie*, fresh "local" products offered by the cheerful and rubicund local farmer, whom we will call "Jeannot" to add a bit of regional colour—all of these are urban myths created purely to draw gullible tourists), I will have to take the DS out of the barn and drive down to Mauriac, in Cantal—though, let us be precise; it is actually a drive "upward", since Mauriac sits at an altitude of 722 metres above sea level, compared to 320 metres for La Charlanne.

I quite enjoy meandering through the aisles of a provincial supermarket with my trolley. Here you can learn so many things about the society of the time; about human nature. And it is an excellent opportunity for a fellow to mingle with people and take the local temperature, as it were, all the while perfecting his guise as a harmless little old man.

I say hello to everyone I pass.

People love the elderly when they are vital and energetic, as a general rule. It reassures them about their own potential futures. Moreover, I always take great care to be well-groomed; appearances are extremely important, especially in the country. Today I am wearing black leather brogues (which I had specially made in England); salt-and-pepper woollen trousers, a light blue linen shirt, a navy cashmere sweater, and a black tweed jacket (I've left my Barbour coat in the car; I'll wear it on the way back, as I'm planning to tour the monastery at La Thébaïde). My red felt hat with the feather in its brim adds a note of whimsy to the classic elegance of my attire. A well-dressed old man shopping for groceries alone could never be suspected of anything but kindliness. They practically argue over who will have the privilege of serving me at the cheese counter. I am happy to play along, taking full advantage of this condescension-tinged cordiality by tasting every variety: "Oh, yes, my dear, I would love to try a bit of this new Bleu des Causses—as long as it doesn't taste like an old shoe, like the Bleu d'Auvergne you gave me last time . . ." (a hint of cantankerousness never does any harm, and indeed only gives the senior in question a bit more "character" . . .).

The young counter assistant, a green-eyed redhead, laughs and blushes most fetchingly; all my cheese-related fantasies are coming true today, it seems. In only a few weeks—that is, since I began gracing this establishment with my weekly presence—I have become the unofficial mascot of Mauriac's new Carrefour supermarket. I grumble at the cashiers as much as I like and they simply give me an indulgent smile. I also take advantage of this quasi-celebrity status to quietly palm a chocolate bar here and there, with full impunity. Were I to be unmasked—were my true identity to be revealed—I know they would be utterly shocked ("I don't believe it; he was such a polite old fellow, dressed nicely and everything! A little strange maybe, but he wasn't a snob!")

I deposit the week's provisions carefully in the DS's capacious trunk: boneless Portuguese sardines, cheese (Cantal de Salers and blue), several loaves of *pain de campagne*, verbena tea, sugar, chocolate, and oranges constitute the staples of my diet. When Lesieur sunflower oil—my preferred brand—is on sale, I buy thirty bottles. I always buy a lot of oil just in case, as it serves the double function of cooking fat and deterrent weapon (in the event of a nocturnal siege of the château). I store most of these bottles in the dungeon, next to a camping stove and a few other useful trifles; this is my panic room—my *chambre forte*—and, in case of attack, I will fight tooth and nail to save my own skin.

I have lingered a bit too long in the supermarket, and now I have the misfortune of encountering a difficulty in the person of Bébert, an old, moustachioed and beret-wearing Cantalian who has considered himself bound irrevocably in friendship to me since we had a brief mycological discussion (on the merits of the *pied de mouton*, or hedgehog mushroom, his favourite, which he insists has the flavour of grilled pork "only better") a few weeks ago at the charcuterie counter. Bébert, as I recall, was trying to determine the exact ingredients of the *boudin blanc* with forest truffles, in the hope that his beloved hedgehog figured among the said "forest truffles". I disabused him of this notion—they were more probably king trumpets, or one might hope so, at least—and provided a few facts about the superiority of the cep.

Since then, every time we meet, Bébert tries to entice me to the local bar, to chat over "a little drop of something"—but I, as you have undoubtedly deduced, am no café-dweller, especially a country café, not least because they invariably feature those horrid umbrellas that, whether open or closed, mimic the various stages of growth of the *Macrolepiota procera*, or parasol mushroom, a lamentably unattractive species. It is inconceivable, therefore, that I could ever be induced to join Bébert in such a place.

Changing the day or time at which I do my shopping has failed to remedy the problem. Bébert, I have realised to my dismay, must loiter outside the Carrefour every day it is open. Since there is no question of my changing supermarkets (for cheese-related reasons, among others; the new Carrefour in Mauriac stocks a remarkable Salers[1]), I have resigned myself. On this particular day, Bébert has news that cannot wait: his grandson discovered a "big basket of morels" yesterday, the first of the season, and we absolutely must go celebrate at the bar. Regrettably, I waste my time attempting to convince him that "morels" do not grow in this region; that these must be *Gyromitra esculenta*, a type of false morel that can be highly toxic and even deadly if not properly cooked for at least ten minutes, with the cooking water discarded afterwards. *Gyromitra* contains a toxin, gyromitrin, which transforms into monomethylhydrazine in the body, which affects the nervous system and the liver by inhibiting the function of vitamin B6—in short, it is extremely unpleasant.

Bébert becomes enraged, swearing to high heaven that he has always eaten these mushrooms, even when he was knee-high to a grasshopper, and that no hoity-toity Parisian is going to tell him what is edible. It is true that the toxicity of *Gyromitra* was only proven relatively recently, in the second half of the twentieth century, and that ancestral customs are im-

---

1 I do not need to tell you, I hope, that the quality of a Salers can be judged by the number of red "stars" near the rind. The more stars, the better.

movably rooted in this remote part of Auvergne. The discussion, which takes place just outside the supermarket's exit, begins to become too animated for my taste; several spectators are observing the scene with interest, and one large lady carrying a basket bulging with imported strawberries has even come to stand immediately beside me, so as not to miss a word of the exchange. Bébert, who has undoubtedly already consumed more than a drop of something, has turned red and, I note with some alarm, looks as if he may be on the verge of a heart attack or stroke, with all the attendant implications of ambulances and paramedics and a possible investigation of the situation. This, I certainly do not need. After all, if it were up to me, the old man could do just as he liked; he could even scarf down his "morels" raw if he chose, which is in fact exactly what I end up advising him to do.

I toss my purchases into the car and depart under the astonished gazes of these countrified fools. Truly, the inhabitants of this region are barely civilized. The Cantalian is a "wild animal and appalling" deep down, to borrow the more general remark made by Schopenhauer on humanity.

Suddenly, I find that I no longer have the heart to stop at La Thébaïde. I content myself merely with checking as I pass to make sure that the monastery's entry gate is locked, and that no strange car is parked in front of it. Then I cross back over the Cantal-Corrèze border via the Saint-Projet suspension bridge, return to La Charlanne, and, after ensuring that my fox-traps have not been set off by any intruders, return to my writing.

According to certain contemporary documents preserved in our library, my great-great-great-grandfa-
ther Aristide had more than one brush with the law
(during the 1760s, roughly the same period as the
Beast of Gévaudan's reign of terror), due to his unfortunate habit of dispatching a series of wives: Marie,
Jacotte, Emeline, and Marie II. A veritable Bluebeard
of La Charlanne, he bumped off these ladies in a manner savage enough to earn himself the contemporary
nickname of Aristide the Bloodthirsty. Who has not
dreamed of visiting—even living in—the Ogre's
Castle? But I have never given any particular credence
to these tales, brutal yet delicious as they are. In fact,
I suspect my great-grand-uncle Firmin, the family's
foremost literary hack, of having actually embroidered
parts of our family tree, to his own liking; it is quite
possible that Uncle Firmin was a true hoaxer, toeing
the line between fact and fiction with the agility of a
tightrope-walker.

"But why would he have done such a thing?" you will
certainly be wondering.

Why, for the matchless pleasure, entirely free and
all the sweeter for it, of hoodwinking everyone. He
undoubtedly cherished the secret hope that no one
would ever find out the truth. The hoaxer is a species
of jokester quite apart; he keeps to the shadows and
has no need of formal recognition. The *frisson* of pleasure he experiences at the thought of having tricked
the people around him—to say nothing of future
generations—into swallowing the most outrageous
nonsense, is his only reward.

What drew my attention to the fictive potentialities of our family tree was its (excessive?) diversity; its abundance, its colour, its dense and bushy quality. It has everything; absolutely everything: murderers (cf. not only the aforementioned Aristide, but also a poisoner, Abigail de la Tournerie, who operated at the turn of the twentieth century; I will return to her later), a long-haul ship's captain, priests (including one of the very first White Fathers, who was later defrocked and roamed a vast part of the African continent as an ethnologist before disappearing somewhere around Timbuktu), scientists, a few madmen, a colonizer (and hero of the Siege of Constantine), an archaeologist who specialized in Gallo-Roman sigils of the Augustan Age and authored a number of resolutely tedious opuscules on the subject, a hack writer (the previously cited Firmin, who clearly put a great amount of care into his own biographical sketch; after all, no one ever serves us better than ourselves), and the inventor of a dubious detector to be used when searching for the *patate du renard*, as it is called in Corrèze, a small, nutty-tasting white tuber named *Conopodium majus* in Latin and, atrociously, *pignut* in English, which can be unearthed in the springtime beneath the leaves of a delicate white-flowered plant. While they are not totally vile, I will confess that I find it extremely difficult to imagine why anyone would dedicate years of his life to inventing a device able to track them. Personally, I would think the idea of a cep-detector much more attractive.

For each ancestor, my great-grand-uncle wrote a more or less detailed biographical sketch. Despite superficial scientific rigor, he allowed himself all sorts of misplaced personal commentaries and interpretations; subjective tangents which are occasionally surprising in their virulence. Here, on the subject of a spendthrift forebear who lived extravagantly on inherited wealth (Alphonse de la Charlanne, 1788-1827, one of Firmin's uncles), the intrepid genealogist lets loose without restraint:

> We, as genealogists, are sometimes called upon to perform the painful task of informing a person's descendants that their ancestor was nothing but an absolute scoundrel, a black sheep, or, even worse, an aberration of the laws of nature. Such is the case with Alphonse René de la Charlanne, who incarnated the family's worst traits in a manner more insidious than I have ever come across since taking on the honorable task of inventorying this historic lineage.

A careful reading of my great-grand-uncle's hysterical indictment reveals that the aforementioned Alphonse, the oldest of ten brothers, had a particular fondness for risqué rave parties (Firmin alludes rather prudishly to "orgies notorious as far away as the Portes du Midi"), good food (with a special predilection for foie gras from Sarlat, which he imported in industrial quantities), and fine wines ("Bordeaux, which he had delivered via barge on the Dordogne in 32-*velte* casks!" gasped his genealo-judge). By the end of his short life, the merry, profligate Alphonse had squandered or drunk up more than two-thirds of the property to which his birthright as eldest son had entitled him—and on this point I must ally myself with the irascible Firmin and condemn him, for if it were possible to restore the Charlanne holdings to their supposed pre-Alphonsian boundaries, I would be in possession today of a large part of the Cantal side of the Dordogne gorges, extending beyond the Saint-Projet bridge and its submerged convent, all the way to La Thébaïde.

I have already mentioned La Thébaïde, I believe. Let me refer you to the enclosed early twentieth-century postcard depicting the convent in question—an eBay find which will undoubtedly fail completely to make you understand the magic of this abandoned place nestled deep in the Dordogne gorges. The convent chapel, which dates from the nineteenth century, is covered with cracks, and the courtyard has become an orchard where pear and apple trees grow among wild herbs and grasses. A short distance away, on the heights above a massive beech tree, a small cemetery has been completely overrun by vegetation. Nuns of a religious order called the Petites Sœurs des Malades were buried there, more than a century ago. The spirit of the forest reigns over La Thébaïde. I go there often, on a woodland pilgrimage during my shopping expeditions to Mauriac—to check on the state of things, as a sort of symbolic owner's tour, and even, occasionally, to discourage any possible tourists (or, worse, mushroom hunters) who might be tempted to ignore the "NO ENTRY" sign posted at the entrance.

※

I am sure the attentive reader will have noticed by now that "nature", in the broad sense of the word, has played a determining role in the development of my personal philosophy. Without slipping into grandiloquent cosmic pantheism or ill-advised neopaganism, let us just say that I have always preferred the company of trees and mushrooms to that of my fellow humans.

"There, all is order and beauty, etc."

Baudelaire was quite wrong when he endorsed the myth of the tropical island thus. A whole slice of literary history should, by rights, be rewritten. He would have done so much better to recover from his youthful excesses in some mossy continental forest— even if only at Fontainebleau or Tronçais. Those are not exceptional forests, I will admit, and the quality of their flora is far below that of the forests of Corrèze and Russia, but they are still worthier than the mostly tropical forests of Reunion Island.

And yet, some misguided notion led General Aupick, Baudelaire's stepfather, to cast him to the four winds in the Southern hemisphere! A soldier's thinking indeed, that. We can at least count ourselves lucky that the trip to India initially planned was cancelled by Baudelaire himself, and that he left La Réunion to return to France double-quick in 1842, less than nine months after his departure—otherwise, *Les Fleurs du mal* would undoubtedly have been cluttered with a mess of orientalist claptrap that would seem quite obsolete to us today. Had I been in the place of his mother and Aupick I would have kept Charles close at hand; no question of sending him to fritter away his time with perfumed beauties. And there was also the option of *la désintox* at Charenton; many people have derived great benefit from this type of institution and emerged virtually unscathed, you know.

Aupick could even have sent his stepson to join in the conquest of the American West, or Alaska, to purge him once and for all of his taste for artificial pleasures. He would have arrived just in time for the Gold Rush; Jack London and Stevenson would have been in for some stiff competition. Everyone would have benefited. To give you a vague idea of the loss to humanity, I refer you to *Incompatibility*. It is not Baudelaire's most well-known poem, or even his best. Written during a stay at Barèges in the Pyrenees, where he had accompanied his mother and Aupick on a cure, it contains the seeds of a true ode to nature, to the towering grandeur of mountains, to lakes and forests—in brief, to the landscapes of the north.

Instead of *Les Fleurs du mal* we might have had *Les Forêts vénéneuses* or *Les Sierras maléfiques*, and I can just see the sonnets dedicated to the great expanses of the Southwest, to the saloon whores, to the towns that popped up along the gold-seekers' trails like so many puffball mushrooms (*Lycoperdon perlatum*). The dissolute Baudelaire would undoubtedly have been tossed in the county jail now and then by a corrupt sheriff; perhaps he would have found himself locked up at some point in Silverton, Colorado, or another such place, but he would have emerged, ever-so-slightly less dandified, to write prose poems about the wild beauty of the American North—or the Southwest; they are virtually the same thing.

Once, it must be a good ten years ago now, I gave a sort of improvised mini-conference on this subject, in the garden-level cafeteria of the Bibliothèque

Nationale. Before a rapidly-growing audience, I put forth the argument sketched above with clarity and conviction. When one of the cafeteria-rats argued strenuously that "Baudelaire wasn't a nature poet," I responded indulgently that he *would have become one.* Baudelaire is a classic case of the poet whose wings were clipped before he left the nest—and the blame for that, at the end of the day, rests squarely on the shoulders of Aupick.

It is a source of personal satisfaction for me to see that "Baudelaire Studies" have missed this point entirely. Yet it is enormously significant.

I could have contributed a great deal to the humanities in general, I believe. Fate decreed otherwise. Destiny can hinge on so little. Perhaps if someone had given Einstein a tennis racket for his seventh birthday, he would be famous today in the annals of Wimbledon for his six consecutive victories in straight sets—which is quite impressive, you must admit, for someone so scrawny . . .

※

But to return to the subject of mushrooms, I would say that, above all, I owe my passion for mycology to the autumnal forest ramblings of my childhood. And the cep very quickly came to occupy a pride of place for me, in both theory and practice. A few educational facts about the cep would not be irrelevant at this stage, I'd wager.

So: The cep, *Boletus edulis* (also *Boletus pinophilus;* the taxonomic differentiation between the two has always seemed pointless to me), is frequently referred to as the "*cèpe de Bordeaux*". This is nonsense. The very best ceps are found in Corrèze; a brief jaunt down the rue Mouffetard or to the Marché Monge in Paris will quickly convince you of this. I am no xenophobe, however, and I will readily admit that very lovely specimens can be found in the Rocky Mountains of America at an altitude of around 3,000 meters, just above the line where groves of aspens (as they call *peupliers trembles* there) give way to alpine prairies covered with shrubs and bilberry bushes—they must be near spruce trees, at any rate, or I cannot hold out much hope for the mycelium. I am telling you all this out of the goodness of my heart, with no expectation of gratitude—there are times when we must contribute selflessly to the general interest. Cep-hunting in this area can yield truly fabulous harvests, on the scale of American enormity; in part, I am sure, because competition is virtually non-existent. Mycologically speaking, the Americans themselves seem to focus exclusively on the giant puffball, a sort of inflatable marshmallow that appears to have been taken straight out of a Disney film.

But I have never personally understood the nickname (I am back on the subject of the so-called cep "de Bordeaux"), which lends itself to confusion. My intuition tells me that a huge misunderstanding lies behind it; an allusion to *colour*, not geographic origin. This is another point to which I'd like to draw your attention: mycological guides and well-intentioned, self-styled "experts" will try to convince you of the edibility of numerous sub-species of boletes (I am thinking particularly here of the *cèpe de bouleaux, Boletus betulicola,* which is orange with a grey stipe or stem, but the *bo-*

let à chair jaune (red cracking bolete) and the *bolet des peupliers* (slate bolete) also come to mind. Resist them at any cost! I will never stoop to gathering such subceps. Only the true cep, the king bolete, *le blanc* (or biely grib [Белый гриб] in Russian, so-named because, unlike inferior boletes, it never blackens or turns blue [or any other one of the eight[1] colours of the rainbow] when cut), is worth harvesting.

My father's example had very little influence on my personal mycological tastes, in the end. And though I do share his passion for ancient mycological books and illustrations, my approach is far less narrow and rigid than his. There has never been any question of shutting myself up in a laboratory to study slides (or mushroom-gills, though the French word, *lamelle*, is the same for both) under a microscope. Rather, I have always viewed mycology from a resolutely multidisciplinary perspective.

The broadness of my mind is undoubtedly what lay behind my profound disagreements with the Société Mycologique de Paris, an organisation of which I was a member for less than one year before being forced to resign. In the very beginning I took myself eagerly to their meetings on the rue Rottembourg, quivering with impatience. To be frank, I hoped those gatherings would capture a fraction of the spirit of Narcisse Théophile Patouillard, one of the founding members of the Société, for whom I cherish a groupie-type admiration: Patou's thesis on hymenomycetes is as gripping as any crime thriller, as is his study on *Les Champignons comestibles et vénéneux de la flore du Jura*

---

1 Not an erroneous number, but new scientific data.

(1883), a well-thumbed copy of which resides in my library at la Charlanne.

All for naught. I was to be deeply disappointed by the narrow views of the Parisian mycologists.

I certainly tried very hard to breathe a bit of originality, a new, stimulating way of seeing and thinking, into the Société. I made multiple attempts to blow the dust off that aging, century-old, hopelessly inward-looking institution. To that end, I had suggested taking some time away from the pointless questions monopolizing the attention of its members (my ex-colleagues were, at that time, obsessed with species as uninteresting as the tomentelloid mushrooms of the Caribbean; two species of the genus Russula (*Russula convivialis* and *Russula rhodomelanea*); *Xeromphalina campanella*; and an uncommon type of heterobasidiomycetes discovered in Burgundy). Instead, I proposed that we concentrate our collective efforts on the cep, which, though well-known and already extensively described and thoroughly taxonomized, remains a species misunderstood and neglected by science.

I was reviled as a fool and summarily kicked out of the Société, with the dismissive instruction to "go back to Corrèze" thrown in for good measure. To add insult to injury, my article on the stipes of ceps (a rigorous and exhaustively documented comparative study of the respective merits of spherical stems versus long and narrow ones, with an unexpected bravura conclusion of the aesthetic superiority of the ovoid stipe) was then rejected twice by the *conseil scientifique* of the *Bulletin de la Société mycologique de France*! Could it be that the name of la Charlanne had reawakened old rivalries or jealousies, unresolved resentments that were really directed at the tomb of my father, a globally recognized specialist on the shaggy ink cap, rather than at me? It is not an impossible theory, and it has never been *dis*proven, in any case. It would certainly explain many things.

✳

But it matters little anymore. I am not bitter. For a long time now, and to my own great benefit, I have taken the side roads; followed a different path. I feel nothing but utter disdain for associative conventions of any type. Unofficial and solitary out of necessity, my contribution to applied mycology remains no less inventive and sophisticated, as you will soon see.

4

Mycology: *the branch of botanical science applied to mushrooms; previously called* mycetology *(1783)*.

Mycology is not a completely harmless discipline, as Count Achilles de Vecchi discovered to his detriment in the State of Washington at the end of the nineteenth century. "Vecchi's Death Said to be Due to a Deliberate Experiment with Poisonous Mushrooms", blared the *New York Times* headline of December 19th, 1897. The unfortunate count had apparently wished to test the various effects linked to the ingestion of *Amanita muscaria*, or the fly agaric. His working hypothesis, specifically, that the toxic properties of this mushroom were greatly overrated, had led him and a colleague, one Doctor Kelley, to ingest *Amanita muscaria* "not in small but in considerable quantities." From then on it was agreed that a fatal dose of fly agaric corresponded on average to fifteen caps (the mind boggles with potential cautionary copy: "Fly agaric: to be consumed in moderation"). The would-be mycologists of the time had no control over their appetites, apparently.

The frontiers of mycology cannot be pushed with impunity, and the *New York Times* article was quick to advocate, with condescension-tinged sagacity, that interested parties join one of the "mycological clubs" which were popping up like mushrooms (ahem) from Boston to New York in those final years of the nineteenth century. Count de Vecchi remains one of the (undoubtedly) very rare victims of *Amanita muscaria*, which is unfortunate, it must be said, for his posthumous reputation; it is almost as ridiculous and unlucky to perish from ingesting a barely toxic mushroom as it would be to die from a toothache in the midst of a plague epidemic.

Amanita muscaria is better known in France by the pleasant popularly-bestowed nickname *tue-mouches*, or "fly-catcher". Its presumed insecticidal properties were first cited in the thirteenth century by Albert le Grand, in his encyclopaedia *De vegetabilibus*:

> "*Vocatur fungus muscarum, eo quod in lacte pulverizatus interficit muscas.*" ("It is called the fly mushroom, for when crushed in milk it kills flies.")

Don't try this at home, *et gardez hors de portée des enfants*.

Though toxic, this magnificent red mushroom with white spots, which flourishes in any forest worthy of the name, whether real or illustrated (I confess a weakness for the fly-catchers of the Russian illustrator Ivan Yakovlevich Bilibin [1876-1942], who never failed to include a multitude of little white-dotted red caps in his otherwise dense, dark, and frightening forests), has questionable lethal properties—with the aforementioned exception of our tragic Italian-American count.

60

If you wish to poison your fellow man, and to do so with mushrooms (a not necessarily unreasonable method), it is advisable to seek out a more reliable member of the genus *Amanita*—of which there are plenty. Besides *Amanita phalloides*, the death cap (a somewhat obvious and lazy choice to my way of thinking), there is *Amanita virosa*, the destroying angel—or, better still, though part of a different genus altogether, there is *Lepiota helveola*, which, to the untrained eye, is as similar to the edible parasol mushroom as one drop of water is to another. A word of advice given at just the right moment, imparted in the confident tones of an expert, can prove immeasurably helpful in cases such as this, and you can always make subtle allusions to the regrettable limitations of your late acquaintance's comprehension skills if the need arises: "No, no, I told him they *weren't* parasols; he misunderstood me *again!*"

To return to our white-spotted agaric, the little clown of the forests: many ethnomycologists have observed its consumption all over the globe. This iconic mushroom can indeed be detoxified. In North America, various accounts prove that the African-American population added it to a vinegar-based sauce after cutting it into thin slices and steaming or boiling it. The same is true in Eastern Europe, Russia, and Japan. One relatively recent study conducted by American researchers, entitled *A Study of Cultural Bias in Field Guide Determinations of Mushroom Edibility Using the Iconic Mushroom, Amanita Muscaria, as an Example* (2008), examines the cultural prejudices to which *Amanita muscaria* has been subjected, and sets about demonstrating that so-called mushroom "guides" are a dubious genre by definition. In the guise of noble scientific and taxonomic study, the authors of these guides go to desperate lengths, it seems, to brand the fly agaric as toxic and even deadly. In short, the culinary redemption of *Amanita muscaria* remains to be accomplished.

In the nineteenth century, there was one man who did make the cause of the fly agaric his hobbyhorse. I am not speaking of the Count de Vecchi, who, as we have seen, forfeited all credibility on the subject; no, I mean my fellow Frenchman, Doctor Félix Archimède Pouchet, a physician and professor of natural history in Rouen, who received part of his medical training under the tutelage of Achille Cléophas Flaubert, father of the famous Gustave. NB: the aforementioned Gustave would draw inspiration from the work of Félix Pouchet on spontaneous generation while writing his historical novel *Salammbô*, and was close friends with the senior Pouchet's son, Georges. In short, the personal-professional and father-son relationships between the Flauberts and the Pouchets were inextricable. And I am sounding a bit like the village busybody, I know—but a great part of the interest in literature, and life, resides in the odd little detail, the amusing coincidence, the snippet of idle gossip, does it not? These things reveal our common humanity, I like to think.

Félix Pouchet's great idea, described in an article published by the *Journal de chimie médicale, de pharmacie et de toxicologie* (1839) ("Experiments on the culinary use of poisonous mushrooms"), consisted of proving that the toxins in many mushrooms, including *Amanita muscaria*, were soluble in boiling water. On these experiments, an ambitious anti-famine plan rested: the large-scale detoxification of poisonous mushrooms would constitute "a great benefit for the poor classes in our country." Pouchet's argument, supported by an analogy with manioc, was implacably logical:

> Manioc, which is a basic nutritive staple for so many peoples, harbours within its tissues the most deadly of poisons; yet man has learned to extract this poison and to use the plant to nourish himself, and we believe that science can do the same for mushrooms.

As a native of Corrèze, a mycologically-rich *département*, I can confirm that Pouchet's plan never really took off. Peasants are both resistant to progress and naturally suspicious (I am not speaking only of old Legrandin here), and I have never come across a single one in the midst of gathering the fly agaric—though, it must also be said, the local peasants generally avoid the forests I choose to frequent. Moreover, at the risk of shocking contemporary sensibilities, I must admit that the good Doctor Pouchet conducted multiple experiments on representatives of the canine species:

> *Boiled, mashed fly agaric = living canine*
> *Bowl of fly agaric broth = dead canine.*

I cannot urge animal-protection associations strongly enough to erect a commemorative plaque in honour of these unknown dogs, collateral victims of a desire—in all other respects perfectly commendable—to put an end to food scarcity in the provinces.

In addition to these dubious scientific-culinary experiments, the versatile fly agaric can be found in numerous mythological and ethnographic tales. The Swedish cartographer Philip Johan von Strahlenberg was the first to describe the shamanic use of this mushroom as he had observed it in the early eighteenth century in Kamchatka, being employed in certain magical rituals. The resulting book, *An Historico-Geographical Description of the North and Eastern Parts of Europe and Asia: But More Particularly of Russia, Siberia, and The Great Tartary: Both in Their Ancient and Modern State* (the English translation in my possession is dated 1738), is accompanied by a rare and precious *Entire New Polyglot-Table of The Dialects of 32 Tartarian Nations; And a Vocabulary of the Kalmuck-Mungalian Tongue.* Philip Johan von Strahlenberg also boasts of having spent thirteen years in captivity in these far-flung regions.

We are certainly within our rights to wonder which parts of the above might have been fabricated by the brave Swedish adventurer during all those years of captivity (apart from his polyglot table of 32 Tatar dialects). Perhaps a moderate use of *Amanita muscaria* helped him to endure the ordeal. I would certainly never cast the first stone at him for it, if so; it is horribly difficult to be deprived of one's freedom of movement. Distractions are indeed necessary. To that end, I once threw myself headlong into philately, an enthusiasm that ended up being of short duration, and I soon abandoned both the fragile things themselves and the profoundly arbitrary and random nature of the discipline: one additional hair in the goatee of Napoleon III can result in colossal variations in value, which is quite ridiculous, as I'm sure you will agree.

Personally, though, it is in the aesthetic sense, above all, that the fly agaric attracts me. I take great pleasure in contemplating its red cap; no cherry, yew-berry (which is far more toxic, by the by), scarlet ibis, or red mullet could claim to rival the carmine brightness of a *tue-mouches* planted against a thick carpet of green moss. As the French naturalist Jean-Baptiste Lamarck so aptly noted in 1815, "this species is remarkable for its beauty." It is, moreover—I am sharing this fact with you in the strictest confidence—*an indicator of ceps*; wherever the fly agaric grows, the cep is not far away (there should be a proverb in this, methinks). I have verified this many times over in the spruce forests of La Charlanne.

✻

I don't know if all this discussion of the edibility of the fly agaric has given you an appetite . . . ?

It certainly has given me one.

But mushrooms are out of the question, since, gastronomically speaking, I loathe them with a passion. Odd as it may seem, my mycological interests are purely aesthetic and scientific in nature. This apparent paradox is undoubtedly worthy of a tangent, but that will have to keep for another day, since it is time for me to put aside today's notes and make for the kitchen.

All is calm outside; the only faint sound is the hooting of an owl somewhere in the Dordogne gorges. The moon, through the kitchen window, looks as if it has been cut into puzzle pieces by the branches of the tallest pine on the property.

I don't think the "visit" will happen tonight. Besides, I left the rifle next to my desk in the large drawing room, and I don't feel the need to go and fetch it during dinner preparations.

❋

I have long been in the habit of cooking for myself, which is useful when one lives in autarky. This way, I am not forced to depend on a sullen, nosy, or preachy cook. Marie came back to work for me for a few months after my mother moved to Creuse (three or four years after my father's death), but I must admit that the cohabitation did not proceed smoothly. Age had embittered her; she muttered constantly under her breath and had to be handled with kid gloves. She talked endlessly about Anastasie in the most outrageously hagiographic terms, and had the further audacity to ask me completely inappropriate questions about old Legrandin (I wonder if she hadn't carried something of a torch for him in her youth) and, in the evenings, after dinner, she had acquired the habit of wandering morosely—and suspiciously—down to the fishpond.

Claiming that I was spending more and more time in Paris, I eventually dismissed her completely, sweetening the deal with a goodly sum to ensure her a comfortable retirement (and assure me of her eternal gratitude). Thus we parted on the very best of terms; I even went so far as to accompany her to the train station in Ussel. Just as she was climbing with astonishing agility into her compartment, I surprised her with one last parting gift: a packet of the dried parasol mushrooms she loved so much.

And so Marie returned to her native Indre, and I never heard anything of her again (I must also admit that I have never been in the habit of following the obituaries in the various regional newspapers too closely).

✳

I am cooking a *truffade*, having procured a good kilo of Cantal cheese in Mauriac—a Salers, of course. Do not settle for inferior appellations, *entre-deux* or *Cantal doux*, which cheesemongers will undoubtedly try to foist off on you, especially if you have the misfortune of being taken for "un Parisien". In a pinch, you may make an exception for *Cantal vieux* or Laguiole. Make no mistake: I adore Cantal, the uncontested king of the famous two hundred and forty-six French cheeses (I am citing the official figure provided by General de Gaulle in a famous witticism; other sources claim that there are between three and four hundred national cheeses extant today). *La truffade* is a dish native to Cantal, based on potatoes and *tomme de Salers* cheese. I have no inclination to provide you with the recipe; after all, this is not a cookbook, and you can look for it yourself. However, I will share with you one of my finds. I have just now come across, in the old kitchen sideboard, a copy of *La Véritable Cuisine de famille par Tante Marie*, a cookbook that was extremely popular in the early twentieth century. I think this copy belonged to my mother, who never used it very much—she always took delight in delegating all culinary tasks to our cook. I don't believe she had much talent for cookery anyway; in any case, I can't remember eating anything prepared by her except for one dish of rice pudding with saffron, which made me ill when I was five or six years old.

I have just been leafing through *Tante Marie*, and have stumbled across the heading "Mushrooms" (this is what I mean about the funny little coincidences in life!), and it is worth quoting:

> **How to pick out good mushrooms.**
> Here is a way of telling if wild mushrooms are good. Cut a large onion into three or four pieces and put them into boiling water with the mushrooms. Let the whole boil for 15 to 20 minutes. If, at the end of this time, the onion has turned black, it is likely that the mushrooms are of poor quality; if the onion remains white, the mushrooms are good.
>
> *Though the above instructions have been relayed to us by a skilled individual, we do not wish to incur any responsibility by recommending them without qualification.*

It occurs to me that my mycological musings, entertaining for the reader though they must be, might have led some of you to mistaken conclusions, so let me be clear: I have never considered using my expertise in mycology for professional purposes. I certainly *could* have, in some situations at least, when the mission required me to first establish a bond of trust with the target. It would then have been relatively easy to slip them a nice heaping spoonful of powdered *Amanita phalloides* (I'd found an entire jar of them, clearly labelled, in my father's laboratory), perhaps in a creamy forest-mushroom soup intended to dazzle the supposed object of my desire. But it was out of the question for me to ride the coattails of the poisoner Henri Girard (I do have my pride), despite his undeniable skill as an herbal bacteriologist. I am speaking, of course, of the Parisian life-insurance profiteer who carried out a series of poisonings via homemade germ culture between 1912 and 1918. He was even—let's not be afraid to say it—a true pioneer in the field, and is known overseas as "the first scientific murderer", a dandy appellation if ever there were one. It is true that his renown was somewhat eclipsed by the subsequent notoriety of another Henri Girard (alias Georges Arnaud, author of *Le Salaire de la peur*—the book, not the film), the gambler/geologist/truck driver/gold-prospector/writer who was acquitted in 1943 of the triple murder of his father, his aunt, and their servant in a Périgord château. I have my own theory about that business, which I will keep to myself, as I do not want to be accused of muckraking.

Our Girard (1875-1921) was, in the words of *Le Petit Parisien*, "a first-rate poisoner who manufactured his poisons himself using the latest formulas in modern chemistry", in the home laboratory he had constructed for that express purpose. Being in possession of these homemade toxic products and germ cultures, he was perfectly positioned to administer precisely the fatal dose to his clients, all with the rather unoriginal aim of cashing in their life insurance policies. His early victims died (or, occasionally, did not) of typhoid fever and suppurating abscesses of all types.

69

Then, frustrated by the inability of these home-grown germ cultures to provide an absolute guarantee of death, Girard turned quite naturally to poisonous mushrooms. Where did he go to collect them, you may ask? To the Jardin du Luxembourg? The Parc Monceau? The Bois de Boulogne? *Le Petit Parisien*, which billed itself as having "the highest circulation of any newspaper in the world", does not linger on this question, crucial though it is. As testament to his change of heart, Girard preserved whole notebooks — which contributed in no small part to his conviction — in which he kept succinct notes such as: *"Mushrooms. Invite Mimiche to dinner."*

"Mimiche", or Michel Duroux, a tenacious type, survived two attempts to poison him with mush-rooms — unlike one Madame Morin, a widow, who was less fortunate, and quickly joined her husband in his final rest.

Though it was not totally reliable, the innovative as-pect of the Girard method was its cleverly subtle use of *Amanita phalloides*. Invited "for an aperitif" (to quote the notebooks) or to dine, his victims never consumed mushroom canapés or omelettes *per se*; rather, the tox-in, skilfully extracted by our amateur bacteriologist, was more probably diluted in a beverage. We must also give Girard his due: as it happens he knew how to make a stylish exit, managing to commit suicide in prison by injecting himself with one of his own germ cultures (most likely typhoid).

However, it would have been in extremely poor taste, I believe, for me to resort to poisoning clients or targets myself.

I am no imitator.

And I have always thought it indispensable to be strictly disciplined, and never to allow the slightest personal preference to infiltrate my professional activities. It is a whole different story, of course, where friends and family are concerned. In these cases it is natural to indulge one's penchants, one's little fixations, one's hobbies. I even choose to see it as the ultimate sign of affection.

My professional signature is as far removed from mycology as possible.

The Nikonor trademark is haemoglobin. At an elevated count.

5

A brief aside here to speak about my sister, for she plays a critical role in this sordid affair.

But, where to start . . . ? What can I say about Anastasie?

I am certain of only one thing where she is concerned: Anastasie, my twin sister, will come here sometime during the next few days and try to kill me. And I am sure she won't be alone. Her disappearance was only a ruse; a ploy designed to trick the adversary. All this time that mygalomorph spider has been lying in wait, crouched in some hole somewhere, watching for the right opportunity to strike, to annihilate me once and for all, *une bonne fois pour toutes.*

I think I would do best to tell it chronologically, at least at first—and only for as long as I choose to, of course.

※

Anastasie was a little girl of average intelligence, merry and rather mischievous, who followed me everywhere like a poodle for the first twelve or thirteen years of our joint existence. To the eyes of an outside observer (such as my parents, for instance), I suppose we were inseparable, as twins so often are in the popular imagination, in children's literature and in reality. It suited me, I won't deny that. I used her, when we played, for all sorts of indispensable tasks I considered unworthy of my superior intelligence: making sure a fir branch could support the weight of a child astride it; assessing the taste and toxicity of an unknown berry; surveying the boundaries of the swamp at the far end of the enormous field behind the château, and trying to cross it with the aid of a judicious arrangement of boards I had devised—something like a raft, but with very long planks placed end to end (the idea had come to me when reading a 1919 edition of *Sinbad the Sailor* with marvellously delicate colour illustrations by Edmond Dulac; when Sinbad is about to be devoured by a giant serpent, you can see the gleam of every greenish scale on the beast, perfectly cut like a jewel). Anastasie very nearly failed to survive that particular experiment, and was only rescued *in extremis* by a hysterical onlooker who had run, shouting, to the château for ropes. Later, when the dramatic tension had eased somewhat, and Anastasie had been dragged out of the swamp like a muddy, howling Venus, I tried to draw my parents' attention to the fact that the "saviour" they had thanked with such humiliating gratitude was nothing but a perfect stranger, an intruder (a *trespasser*, I hurled in English at my mother), blatantly disobeying the laws regarding private property; in short, what was he doing on our land, when he was so willing to risk his life saving damsels in so-called distress? My unimpeachable childish logic unleashed a storm of maternal wrath that was both savage and,

I must say, greatly misplaced. I was sent to my room and put on bread (well, *brioche*, actually) and water for two days, a flagrant injustice for which I took years to forgive my parents.

But "à quelque chose malheur est bon,"[1] as our cook Marie used to be fond of saying (she was a great collector of trite clichés).[2] The incident had the effect of teaching me to be circumspect, and leading me to the inescapable conclusion that Anastasie was an untrustworthy character with whom I should have as little to do as possible in future.

In any case, my intellectual precociousness meant that I soon favoured intensive sessions of reading over wild games and trout-fishing expeditions with my sister. Despite our shared birthday, I was so far ahead of her in every branch of knowledge that you would have assumed me to be older by several years. The only tutor who dared to question this judgment was forced to resign in disgrace only a few months after his arrival—but that is a grim story which has nothing at all to do with our business here, and is hardly worthy of a narrative detour.

In a word, Anastasie had nothing more to offer me.

---

1 The French equivalent of "every cloud has a silver lining".
2 "Don't knock it until you've tried it" was another often-repeated favourite of hers, trotted out whenever I reminded her that I hated mushrooms and would never consent to try them. Anastasie, during this period, was in the habit of stuffing herself with parsleyed parasol mushrooms beneath Marie's approving gaze. I have often wondered if this wasn't the true cause of my aversion—purely culinary, I remind you again—to mushrooms.

Who knows what she thought of this revelation; perhaps she saw it as a betrayal, a cruel rejection, a kind of fratricide. Perhaps she was bored to tears, thus deprived of her playmate, the uncontested leader of all our joint activities. There can be little doubt that my unceasing inventiveness, my Verne-inspired scientific imagination, my natural ingenuity, must have seemed irreplaceable to her. Really, I had withdrawn—without fully realizing it—the star that had illuminated her whole childhood, and, in a way, I can understand what she must have felt. She must have suffered greatly. And when she tried to have me locked up the first time, I can see now that it was the bitter gesture of a little girl abandoned by the older brother she adored and admired so much. I could have buried the hatchet, as Marie used to say (though always with a frown that belied her pacifist words). But Anastasie has shown an obstinacy, a vindictive pugnacity, that has only grown worse with the years, and which I cannot ignore for much longer. She has rummaged through the dirty laundry of the past to mount, with meticulous, obsessive hatred, a case against me. And every indication now leads me to believe that she intends to make an attempt on my life.

※

I am not the type to blame everything on the parents at any cost. They are not responsible for all of it; they tried their best and, I believe, managed the situation with tact and sensitivity. Though they must have been fully aware of my exceptional gifts, they never openly gave Anastasie cause to sense her inferiority. I can

75

even remember times when they clearly took her side (cf. the swamp fiasco).

Our education at home, which may have seemed rather old-fashioned and anchored in the previous century to our contemporaries' way of thinking, was nevertheless robust and of high quality. My mother took charge of our linguistic development; I have been fluent in the language of Agatha Christie, Dickens, and Shakespeare (in order of preference) since my earliest youth, and apparently speak with a terribly *posh* accent, which made me the (temporary) butt of everyone's jokes during my sojourns on the other side of the Channel. My mother's family—repressed, conservative, and totally *bonkers* as only the English aristocracy can be (hadn't they married my mother off to an obscure little Corrèze country squire purely to annoy a Francophobic neighbour? That, at least, is the version of the story I heard when I was there) even insinuated ironically that I was more Royalist than the Queen. I must have inherited my gift for languages from my mother; in addition to her native tongue, she spoke Russian and a French that was rich and precise, just faintly dotted here and there with an occasional Anglicism. *Tout à fait charmant*, if you ask me. It is also to my mother that I owe being spared from boarding school, when I reached the appropriate age. She understood that my sensitive, artistic nature could not have borne the rigours and bullying that are every boarder's lot in life. My father's timid mentions of the small seminary at Saint-Flour were likewise vigorously rejected, to my intense relief.

Once the danger of school was past, the rest of my childhood and adolescence proceeded in peace and serenity. I discovered Chateaubriand at the age of around fourteen and spent a whole year reading *Les Mémoires d'outre-tombe, Atala, René,* and *Les Aventures du dernier Abencérage* in a nook above the dungeons that I had specially fitted out with blankets, pillows, candles, and even an old Persian rug with a dark red pattern, which I had convinced my mother to give me (in exchange for a promise to work assiduously every morning with Monsieur Feuillère, the unfortunate tutor I believe I have already mentioned). Visitors were strictly prohibited; this was, after all, a retreat, a private space, dedicated to a sacrosanct activity requiring uninterrupted concentration and solitude: reading. I had informed Anastasie, in particular, that her appearance would trigger the release of my trained spiders—only a charming adolescent joke, of course, but her infinite gullibility and cowardice tipped the balance in my favour, and my sanctuary remained inviolate.

These readings had a great impact on my sensitive soul. It was impossible for me not to notice the obvious parallels between François-René, or his fictional double René, and myself. Didn't I, like him, spend "each autumn [and winter, spring, and summer, in my case] at the paternal château, located amid forests, near a lake [a carp pond, for me], in a remote province"? Naysayers would probably point out the fact that the "paternal château" of Combourg was undoubtedly ten or twenty times grander than La Charlanne (which is no small fry itself among Corrèze's manorial castles, by the way), but they will never understand that it is the *atmosphere* that counts, a common breeding-ground, conducive to the accomplishment of great things. Combourg, la Charlanne: same difference!

I also shared with François-René a love of forest rambles in gloomy weather; "a melancholy turn of mind led [me] deep into the woods," too. On that note, I must add that, bizarrely in the eyes of a mycologically-inclined reader, there is no reference to that subject in Chateaubriand. I know that Bretagne is no mushroom paradise, but it is still disappointing. With his affinity for the autumn, he must have sometimes come across a bolete, or a carpet of *trompettes de la mort*. He could have made some descriptive effort; French literature would be the better for it today. Upon reflection, I would bet—distracted melancholic dreamer that he was—that he must have crushed a fair few mushrooms in his day (I am speaking of ceps in particular), which casts François-René de Chateaubriand, his characters, and the Romantic movement in a whole new, more dubious—even controversial—light.

I could have forgiven that, but, despite the numerous similarities to which I referred earlier, there was something about Chateaubriand that made me uncomfortable: the role played by Lucile, or her fictional double Amélie. For example:

> [...] I found ease and contentment only in the company of my sister Amélie. A sweet similarity of temperament and tastes bound me closely to this sister; she was slightly older than myself. We loved to scramble up hillsides together, and sail on the lake, and roam the woods when the leaves fell; indeed, the memory of those walks still fills my soul with pleasure. [*René*]

For a long time I was torn between anger and jealousy. When all was said and done, it seemed that, despite the resemblances and affinities, there was an impassable gulf between us (a remark that also applies to Anastasie and me, as it happens). (François-) René did not know what it was to endure, day after day, the presence of a vicious, evil-minded harpy. I have taken the liberty of remedying the situation by adapting Chateaubriand's prose—which has the double advantage of reflecting my own reality and introducing the mycological note so glaring by its absence in the viscount's oeuvre:

> I found only discomfort and unhappiness in the company of my sister Anastasie. An ineffable difference in temperament and tastes separated me forever from this sister, though she was my twin. It was no easy task for me to wander the rye fields, fish for trout in the rivers, or search the autumn forests for that most royal of its denizens, the cep, in her company; these memories fill my soul with bitterness even now.

I am resolved, however, to end on a conciliatory note. Certain snippets from Chateaubriand, which I have just come across while rereading the testamentary preface of *Les Mémoires d'outre-tombe*, have stirred a deep echo in me as I, too, approach the final watershed moment of my life:

> When the veil of death descends be-
> tween me and the world, the drama of my
> life will be seen to have been divided into
> three acts . . .

And Chateaubriand goes on to enumerate his three "successive careers" as a traveller, a writer, and a statesman. We know which of the viscount's three acts posterity has chosen to remember. But it is with some trepidation that I ask myself which of my own three, the mycologist, the writer, or the . . . consultant, I will call it, for the sake of expediency, will leave its mark on the planet?

✳

When did I first begin to write? It's difficult to put my finger on a precise date and, tragically, my secret journal—which could have shed some light on the question for us—has been lost for more than seventy years. At least I escaped the curse that has become so terribly widespread in the context: the temptation to produce "youthful poetry". That pitfall avoided, I launched myself headlong into dense, rather opaque and symbolist prose which owed a good deal, when I think about it, to Gracq's *Le Château d'Argol*, which prominently featured impenetrable forests and shadowy characters with heightened emotions who loved, deceived, and tortured each other before stabbing one another to death and/or committing suicide by drowning in murky lakes filled with hygrophilic plants.

As I gave myself over to these innocent yet promising literary occupations, Anastasie busied herself with pursuits of her own. I began to be aware of small details—an insolent glance intercepted; subtle changes in her behaviour and that of the new tutor, Monsieur Feuillère—which led me to suspect that she was in league with him against me.

✳

We must have been thirteen or fourteen years old when it became urgently necessary to get rid of a tutor, whose predecessor had packed his own bags and fled in the space of a few hours one day, without demanding the money owed him or giving my parents the least hint of any explanation worthy of the name. We could only watch, dumbstruck, as Monsieur Brisquette crammed two battered suitcases into the trunk and sped off, tires squealing, in his rickety Citroën 2CV. We never saw him again.

Of course, by that time I had already attained a more-than-adequate level of erudition. I therefore suggested to my parents that I could manage the rest of my education on my own. The château's library, as I have said many times, was admirably suited for this type of exercise. My mother and father, I continued, were certainly free to hire someone to deal with my featherbrained sister if they wished, but I thought it an utterly pointless financial investment, a pure waste of time and money, *un gros gâchis*. The conversation turned nasty, and Anastasie gripped me by the neck in an (extremely convincing, I tell you) attempt to strangle me. My sister never did manage to master social etiquette, those little unsaid things so essential if one wishes to fit in with the crowd, which enable reasonable people to exchange differing opinions without resorting to blows.

My father, furious, quickly separated us and announced that, *primo*, he would not tolerate brawling among his progeny, and *secundo*, it was out of the question for my formal learning to be discontinued. He and my mother would move heaven and earth to find us a replacement tutor as quickly as possible. Our education was sacrosanct, and it was up to him, Pierre de la Charlanne, to ensure that *blah blah blah* . . .

※

And so it was that Monsieur Feuillère, Parisian by birth, *corrézien* by adoption, made his appearance at the château de la Charlanne one spring day, armed with a stack of letters of recommendation, each one more laudatory than the last. He had taught for more than a decade at the Lycée Voltaire de Paris and now wished, for obscure health reasons, to "be somewhere green". He hoped to dedicate himself henceforth to the private education of young and brilliant minds, and was thrilled by the thought of the stimulating discussions he would have with Anastasie and me on subjects as varied as algebra, geometry, history, literature, and the applied sciences. Such pedagogical zeal did not augur well, but Monsieur Feuillère would undoubtedly have remained just one name on the long list of tutors who had sojourned briefly at the château de la Charlanne, had it not been for his unnatural alliance with Anastasie.

Feuillère annoyed me from our very first lesson, when he insisted that Anastasie and I take an identical general knowledge test—an innovative examination he had developed himself, as he made sure to tell us. Apparently he was also the author of a *Nouvelle grammaire latine*, which had won some prize or other three years earlier. There was no end to the man's vanity.

I had made sure to tell him about the immeasurable lead I enjoyed over my mediocre twin. He would have to split himself pedagogically and find some teaching materials of a different calibre altogether if he wanted to keep me from stagnating in the swamp of underachievement in which Anastasie was hopelessly mired.

The results of the aforementioned test reassured me in the thought that the letter sent to Brisquette, his predecessor, had been a grave error.

This letter had been the fruit of a particularly idle afternoon, of the sort with which every teenager of yesteryear will be familiar. I don't know how the idea came to me, but suddenly I found myself writing a series of relatively crude and explicit declarations, signed with Anastasie's name. In this document, if I recall correctly, she said that she wished to hold in her hands and stimulate Brisquette's manhood, which she imagined was still vigorous (a few small but fairly successful sketches illustrated these remarks). She further proposed coming to him in his bedroom at nightfall, in order to offer him her virginity and to give herself over, without restraint, to passionate embraces which would have made an adept of the Kama Sutra blush.

I look back today on these schoolboy amusements with nostalgia-tinged indulgence. Boys will be boys.

I could certainly not have predicted Brisquette's regrettable oversensitivity, nor the snowballing repercussions of this playful missive, starting with the rushed departure of a tutor who had not, after all, been overly troublesome. But what impetuosity—what haste—in Brisquette! Was he merely afraid, or was the fear that he would not be able to resist Anastasie's temptations? My sister was already quite beautiful then, breathtakingly so, in fact; I will say that much for her.

All of this is to say that I did not get on with Monsieur Feuillère. He had clearly given preference to Anastasie and, with that, chosen the camp of eternal losers. Too bad for him.

His departure became a matter of urgency.

When I wasn't absorbed, in my dungeon, in writing Gracq-inspired pastiches, I dedicated most of my mental energy to this pressing matter. A passionate letter signed with Anastasie's name would not do this time; it would be much too dangerous, given the obvious complicity that already existed between those two sinister individuals.

I thought briefly of resorting to one of my special concoctions; I was at that time carefully cultivating a small patch of hemlock, hidden behind the tombstone of Valérien de la Charlanne (15?-1630). Nothing on an industrial scale, you understand; but I had already been pleased to observe the appearance of several white umbels, signalling a successful harvest. Here again, though, the risk was too great. My father might drag himself away from his slides long enough to notice strange symptoms, to contest the Grivaudian diagnosis of indigestion-leading-to-death, and, *worst case scenario*, to have a toxicological analysis conducted by the laboratory in Tulle! No, I could not permit myself such a lapse; my "gentian" root-based culinary experiments were undoubtedly still too fresh in everyone's mind.

✳

Still, I lacked neither imagination nor resources, and Monsieur Feuillère did indeed end by returning to Paris *en compagnie de* his *Nouvelle grammaire latine*, less than five months after his triumphal arrival in Limousin.

The bracing air of the Corrèze countryside is not for all Parisians; Monsieur Feuillère had overestimated his sturdiness. A man of dubious morals, he had disgraced himself as a pedagogue and an instructor by attempting to lure a brilliant but impressionable young man (your humble servant) off the straight and narrow path. My father's fury was implacable, and the tutor packed off with quasi-Brisquettian speed.

Anastasie, profoundly disgusted by the whole immoral business, asked to continue her education at the convent in Ussel. Her request was granted. But I believe that she remained forever bitter toward me after this episode, whether consciously or not.

✳

The château de la Charlanne was finally restored to the idyllic tranquillity that characterized it at the best of times, and I was able to return peacefully to my own pursuits.

6

I just went to make sure the briefcase is still in the large wardrobe in my bedroom, concealed behind piles of ancient bed-linens embroidered with the initials of one of my forebears, A.C. On my way from the kitchen, I had seen traces of mud on the wooden floor that worried me a bit. Then I remembered that it had rained a good deal the night before and that, in my hurried return from Mauriac, I must have forgotten to take off my imported, black leather English brogues. Reassured, I came to sit in the *cantou*. The fire is almost out; only a few glowing cinders remain. Despite my vigorous assertions to the contrary, I have never learned to make a fire. It takes me a good dozen matches and two bundles of very dry old issues of *La Vie corrézienne* to raise a flame.

I surprise myself by missing good old Rufus (our servant); he may not have been the sharpest tool in the box but he could make a fire like no one else. The poor fellow was the victim of a deadly fall when I was around ten years old. The double ladder on which he was standing to repair a dormer had apparently slipped, and he had smashed his skull on one of the stone lionesses in the courtyard.

My parents were devastated by the incident, much more so than I would have expected, and decided by mutual agreement not to replace Rufus. Anastasie also decided just then to put on a performance of her own, and was seized in the courtyard by a series of ill-timed spasms, in the best hysterical tradition[1]. Between fits of uncontrollable sobbing, she even accused me, without coming right out and saying it, of having pushed the ladder. My parents, thank goodness, did not give any credence to these outrageous calumnies, but here again, we can see the first indications of a growing instability that would burst fully into life in the years to come.

Enough of that; the fire now consists of a healthy bunch of flames licking a lovely large, dry beech log, so I can return to my writing in peace.

As I had feared, my first weeks and months in Paris were rather laborious, for various, lamentably unoriginal reasons: for one thing I had a noose around my neck, financially speaking; my parents had proven themselves to be distressingly backward-thinking when it came to money. Furthermore, I had been sent to lodge in the home of a distant cousin who lacked

---

1 I refer you on this subject to the key writings of Charcot à la Salpêtrière; his 1882 work *Sur les divers états nerveux déterminés par l'hypnotisation chez les hystériques* is utterly conclusive on this point: it is textbook Anastasie.

even the smallest drop of blue blood, and who monitored my comings and goings with disapproval and suspicion. I decided very quickly not to stay and rot away in that insalubrious residence, which would have made Balzac's *pension* Vauquer a contender for hotel of the year in comparison.

Regular frequentation of the law school was an unacceptable option. Once the enrolment period was at an end, I ceased all contact with the University. I must have gone there only three or four times at most, just to get a feel for the place. The rare lectures I attended on those occasions were utterly mind-numbing. Clearly, my destiny did not lie in the slow and patient elucidation of arcane laws.

It was time for a career change.

If I had not met Vilerne, things could have gone quite badly for me. To this day, I consider him a sort of fairy godmother, a guardian angel sent to watch over me at a time of personal doubt, uncertainty, and despair. When I was forced to separate myself from him—for principally ethical-aesthetic reasons; I will return to the point if I have time—it was not without some regret. But, after all, everyone knows that sometimes one must kill fairies and father-figures. And I had begun to feel a sort of acute *anxiety of influence*[1], which only vanished when my mentor—that is really the term that best describes him—was out of the way (attention: euphémisme!).

---

1 See the excellent book by the American literary critic Harold Bloom on the subject.

Every large city has its Vilerne. He is not difficult to find; all you have to do is frequent the shady areas where nocturnal travellers, disaffected thugs, and aging prostitutes cross paths. I needed money. My options were limited. Without flinching and with, I believe, a great deal of professionalism, I completed the first task given to me by an uninteresting small-time hood. From bit players to minor associates, I made my way up the food chain until I reached the great white shark. It took me less than three months.

Vilerne's physical appearance didn't match what he was, which was a considerable asset. A tireless gossipmonger with a fondness for *andouillettes* and the martial arts, he looked as if he would have been more at home in a 1960s French comedy film than at the head of an international criminal organization. We got along well, at least at first, and I quickly made myself indispensable for liquidation operations of all types.

Business really began to thrive once I moved to the 5th arrondissement, into a small apartment in the Quartier des Gobelins, just off the Place Saint-Médard. I had cut ties with the law school some time before, though the reports sent regularly to Corrèze gave detailed accounts of my various academic successes as well as my first forays into the legal profession. My mother died convinced that at least half of her progeniture had "gone up to Paris" to find success—and in this she wasn't wrong.

Vilerne and I met each morning at around nine o'clock in a café on the avenue des Gobelins. After devouring his croissants and carefully licking two or three buttery fingers, Vilerne would flick a malicious glance at me and open a crumpled, grease-stained black notebook. "Hmm, let's see if we have anything for Nikonor today . . ."

He revolted me with his faux doting-uncle mannerisms, his medical-secretary routine. I played it *très cool*, face expressionless, hyper-professional; I had practiced carefully in the mirror to perfect my demeanour, and more than one would-be killer has imitated my stone-faced imperturbability since those days, with varying degrees of success. I have a weakness for Alain Delon in *Le Samouraï*, and it wouldn't surprise me to learn one day that he borrowed the Nikonor look from the Parisian underworld of the nineteen-fifties . . .

Vilerne would eventually hand over my assignment; it was almost always a nocturnal one. Actually, I had set out the *sine qua non* condition that my afternoons must be kept free. Vilerne had grumbled at first that I was acting like a prima donna, and it's true that it was a risky demand, since I was only a beginner—a talented one, certainly, but a beginner nonetheless. He had given in, in the end. In this way I was able to spend every afternoon at the Bibliothèque nationale on the rue de Richelieu, imbibing in small doses those nineteenth-century literary masterpieces that weren't on our shelves at home.

The austere scholarly atmosphere of the reading room had impressed me deeply; I felt myself to be in communion with the place, and was proud to be part of the charmed circle, the *happy few*, who had rejected the activities of our contemporaries to sacrifice ourselves on the altar of Knowledge—at least, that was how I saw things at the time. The profligate *Fumistes* of the *fin de siècle* enchanted me above all: Alphonse Allais, Charles Cros, Maurice Rollinat (author of poetry that might be vaguely offensive to some, but which amused me greatly; see for example his joyous rallying-cry: "Ah! To smoke opium from a baby's skull/Feet propped carelessly on a tiger . . . "). I even toyed vaguely with the idea of writing a doctoral thesis—and, why not, of teaching at the Sorbonne in my free time once I had done so—but my preliminary discussions with a professor with an eye to defining a potential subject proved disappointing, and I gave the project up rather quickly. It was during this period that I attempted, under a false name—for my professional future was at stake, and if Vilerne had caught wind of the affair my reputation would have been ruined—to publish an article on Maurice Mac-Nab's *poêles mobiles*, or "movable stoves"; in it I demonstrated with panache the profoundly allegorical nature of the *poêles* in question. The article, though never published, has aged rather well, if I do say so myself; especially when compared to the current obsolescence of so-called structuralist pieces written in the same era.

With regard to my extra-literary activities, I quickly found myself with a reputation as a diligent and professional clean-up man. And when I struck out on my own, three or four years after my arrival in Paris, a good number of Vilerne's clients decided to follow me (it's rather like the medical profession that way; the main thing is to build up a loyal clientele, and then business comes by itself via word of mouth). This hard-won independence contributed to my financial prosperity at least as much as it did to my personal fulfilment. I am a lone wolf by nature. I made the mistake of taking on a partner only once, and the attempt ended in an abject failure—one from which my associate did not recover.

Over the course of my long career, I evolved in most sectors of activity with the ease of a Hiroshige carp in the family pond: politics and the public sector; unions; the mafia; small and medium-sized businesses; large companies; the cultural sector; tourism and travel; psychiatric institutions and hospitals; information technology; banks, prisons; insurance; the arts; television; print media; fashion; real estate; drug trafficking; marketing and communications firms; arms trafficking, etc. This brought me into contact with every type of person and every stratum of society (I am speaking of both clients and targets).

It was quite enriching. I learned a great deal.

I also gained a wide array of the socio-professional skills most highly prized on the job market, particularly having to do with public relations:

Development of trust- and esteem-based relationships with a varied clientele (as mentioned above).

It is essential, for a contractor such as myself, to be able to work with as much ease and facility for the wealthy Paris banker who has come to find his wife (or mistress) irritating or inadequately decorative, as for the small-time crook in the red-light district seeking to monopolize his patch.

Ability to manage one's actions and to find alternate solutions when unexpected events crop up.

For example: knowing how to bounce back when a certain brand of bin-bags—which has since gone bankrupt; justice does exist—fails you and causes you to leave a trail of undesirable debris in the garden of a target as you return to your vehicle. Moreover, I loathe waste, and always try as hard as possible to conserve resources. Improvisation does not necessarily have to mean leaving chaotic sprays of blood *à la* Jackson Pollock.

Strategic positioning of business in its environment.

I fear this is a mere euphemism. In my field, positioning often requires eliminating the competition, pure and simple. Any methods are then acceptable. I have occasionally resorted to decentralization, and managed the business from my base in Corrèze, but the principle remains the same, once you are recognized as a *brand name*.

Establishment of and adherence to a budget.

I have always followed budgets, sometimes literally to the other side of the globe, when a cardboard yakuza, relieved of an enemy thanks to my good and loyal services (a tenacious type on whom the Nikonor gimlet[1] had no effect, if memory serves; I was forced to resort to an infinitely less sophisticated method with some gardening tool or other), attempted to disappear without paying my fee. Financial rigour is vital in business. I have never given a single *centime* of credit to anyone.

---

1 A refined technique unanimously recognized by specialists today as the most reliable method of minimizing blood spatter. I want to draw your attention here to the fact (which will undoubtedly surprise many of you) that I have always used my true first name in my profession. Just because we work in a highly specialized and covert field, doesn't mean that we make absolutely everything up. My first name has a certain Slavic, vaguely menacing quality that is perfectly suited to my brand image. And, of course, no one has ever imagined for a second that it could be anything other than a pseudonym.

*Formation (*or dissolution*) of networks.*

In the context of his various fields of operation, a contractor such as myself knows how to assemble and use a portfolio of contacts by regularly updating information about the different members of his network. It was in disassembling one such network that I was forced to make the difficult (but so necessary!) decision to separate myself from the aforementioned partner—not to be confused with Vilerne; they had completely opposite personalities. The former was taciturn and surly and possessed almost no social skills, to the extent that he ended up doing serious harm to our customer relations management (CRM).

Ability to monitor and anticipate, in order to remain informed and identify new developments in the field of operation.

Let me simply say here that one does not remain at the head of an organization such as mine for more than half a century *par hasard*. Monitoring and anticipation are vitally important and, even though my activities have now been reduced to the bare minimum, I continue to carry out these functions today.

On that note, I have just completed my guard duty; the fox-traps have not been touched. I noticed nothing unusual. The molehills which recently appeared in the meadow have proven, upon inspection, to be quite real. I think I shall be able to *dormir sur mes deux oreilles* tonight—or *sleep on both ears*; it is not often that the French and English expressions match quite so closely.

In short, I was, and I remain today, a highly qualified individual, a true professional, and during those formative years in Paris I quickly established a number of principles and precepts for myself from which I have never deviated. I am sometimes asked about the secret of my success; what has guided my professional choices and led to my reputation for perfectionism. I always reply that the first rule is silence. Any idle chatter, misplaced confidence, or exchange with anyone at all is in extremely poor taste and the equivalent of signing your own death warrant. Entering this profession means making a vow of silence, taking holy orders. *Ni plus, ni moins.*

My second rule is the following: I never judge my clients. They all have their reasons. I believe everyone has the right to rid himself of his fellow man (or men). The Americans understand that very well. That country is unfairly criticized too often in France; they do not joke around, for example, with the free circulation of weapons of every kind there. And there are many perfectly capable Americans who exercise their highest civil and constitutional right in public places. Too bad for the victim, who should have thought of that solution first. Survival often hinges on reaction speed, on base instinct and the ability to adapt to one's environment. It is not for *sissies*.

Rule number three is to control the whole chain of production. Never delegate or entrust the smallest part of the process, however trivial it seems, to a third party. You must admit that finding a truly trustworthy person is a challenge indeed.

And, last but not least, you must be able to lie fluently, under any circumstances. Dissimulation is an art I mastered very early on. I possess an unsurpassed talent for pulling the wool over people's eyes. I have persuaded many, many people to swallow absolute whoppers (I prefer the phrase: *avaler des couleuvres*, to swallow grass-snakes), starting with my immediate family. Even the men in white coats have been persuaded to accept any number of outrageous tales. They have always ended up letting me go.

They had to.

They could never prove a thing.

I have slipped between their fingers like an eel more than once. I've often found it greatly amusing to do so. I know all of their jargon, and it is child's play for me to turn their own idiotic methods against them; to feign the sort of "improvement" which encourages hope for "a successful progressive reintegration into family life and society."

✳

Of course, I cannot claim to be totally infallible, and I make no attempt to conceal the fact that some of the lessons I have learned have been painful and bloody ones, as I have seen written in certain sensationalist publications. In the earliest of the photo albums documenting my activities, I have entitled one such event *The Failure at the Pink House*. Practically a Simenon title, wouldn't you say?

I had just struck out on my own professionally, so I wasn't a complete greenhorn, but the mission went very wrong and, had it not been for my presence of mind, it might even have proven fatal.

Everything had begun according to plan. There was no indication, absolutely none at all, that I might hit a snag. I had approached the operation without a hint of unease or apprehension, with no intuitive misgivings that would have cast a shadow over the events to come. Though I give no credence whatsoever to the psychoanalysis of dreams, I do believe strongly in the power of dreams themselves; I have rescheduled or delayed an action or a journey more than once on the heels of some striking nocturnal vision, a policy that once enabled me to escape—just barely—from a particularly unexpected attempt at capture. I won't tell you the rest of that story either; I am no stool pigeon, and will confine my remarks, as far as possible, only to what is strictly necessary.

To return to the subject of my dreams: they are usually vivid, extremely dense, and wildly creative. I subscribe to the theory that the brain, that mischief-maker, is like a toolbox which sleeps, can reorganize at will, without rhyme or reason, and that one dreams in accordance with his intellectual and/or artistic capabilities. For my part, I have often regretted not being able to record my dreams; my nocturnal visions rival Hitchcock's greatest films in terms of colour, detail, direction, and suspense. With modern technology that sort of dream-camera might well not be far off in the future, but it will be too late for me; I will have missed the boat and the Oscar for best director of dreams.

Each mission, you must realize, requires meticulous preparations that proceed according to a pre-established ritual. Diligence, discipline, and security of execution (no pun intended) lie at the heart of a system that is quasi-military in its precision. In this case, I had completed all the necessary research. I was good and ready. It had taken me a full three weeks to compile an exhaustive casefile on the target and his family. I knew everything about him, from the type of wine he liked best (Châteauneuf-du-pape) to the time of day he took his shower (in the morning, after a cup of Ricoré); from his wife's brand of perfume (Pomme d'Amour by Nina Ricci) to the name of his daughter's Barbie doll (Victorine). I knew what day and time the garbage collectors came; which dog food they gave Rico (Canigou), and that Rita (the maid) was about to disappear with her mistress's jewellery.

When the final mission order had come through (single target, family to be spared), I had dressed in shabby, comfortable old clothes and espadrilles and put in the tinted contact lenses that masked my eyes, which are the colour of *myosotis*—forget-me-nots, in English; in short, I made sure I was as unmemorable as possible. Handsomeness isn't always an asset in this line of work. I drove the most innocuous car I could find, its trunk previously loaded with the brief-case containing the tools of my trade, methodically sharpened and carefully checked before each mission: gimlet, axe (for big jobs), butchering instruments (boning knife and slicers), cleaver, saw, scraper. Disabling the alarm system with its link to the police station had been ridiculously easy, and I had had no problems crossing the wooded grounds typical of the Versailles middle class, at the back of which stood a large 1920s residence coated in gaudy pink pebbledash. I knew the place as well as the pockets of the Barbour jacket I'd left back at home, from the dozen garden gnomes that dotted the lawn to the imposing front doorbell that rang loud enough to burst an eardrum—though it wouldn't on this day.

I slipped into the living room via the rear bay window, as planned. From there, I made my way to X's office. He should have been there alone; every piece of information I had gathered pointed to it, and the variables (X's post-prandial occupations ranged from the attentive "reading" of *Playboy* to the balancing of his chequebook) had been accounted for again and again.

There is no point in denying that what occurred next owed a great deal more to improvisation than it did to careful planning. Murder can happen just that quickly. Even today, more than half a century later, I cannot look at a garden gnome without reliving that traumatic experience in all its sordid brutality.

Everyone has his *madeleine*, I suppose. I have no right to complain about mine.

The headlines to which the whole unfortunate business gave rise did no credit either to the perspicacity of the police or to that of the French press: "Family massacred amid garden gnomes: Bloodbath blamed on a prowler who took flight": "Butchery in Versailles: Police tracking garden gnome thief caught in the act"; "Garden gnome carnage: investigation now focusing on psychiatric institutions".

It was a serious blunder, and it required me to flee to England for several months. My contacts were interrogated, and I was *persona non grata* in Paris. I decided to be a good sport about the thing, and make the most of the situation. Every great man has known the pain of exile. I considered the ordeal as a certificate of authenticity; a rite of passage for a true creative genius who, unrecognized in his own time, will be venerated by generations to come.

I also took advantage of the opportunity to explore London and refamiliarize myself with the dialect. Out of sheer idleness, I even made a touristic pilgrimage in the footsteps of Jack the Ripper, a killer of the lowest calibre, of whom the British have no right to be so proud.

Next, I took the time to visit my mother's family. You will undoubtedly complain that it was not very original of me, but I will say this: it is good, at times of existential crisis or doubt, to be able to turn to those closest to you; to go back to the source, to essentials. It is also important to put one's own house in order before making a run at anyone else's. At the end of the day, I can pride myself on always having put family first.

7

Cruel fate, merciless in its pursuit, decreed that my mother and her second husband would perish in conditions and agonies not dissimilar to those that had taken my father a decade earlier. I had visited them not long before, at their home in Creuse. My mother had seen fit to take a bumpkin from that region as her second husband, the owner of a large farm near Ahun—not to be pronounced Ah-oon, as a non-French-speaker of my acquaintance persists in doing (one who remains, despite repeated lengthy stays in the country, obdurately ignorant of the French language in all its aspects, from lexical to grammatical to phonetic).

Unlike my sister, who had ceased giving any sign of life at that point, I had graciously made a habit of bringing them a bounty of *produits corréziens* once per year, mainly in the form of fresh and/or dried mushrooms (it must be acknowledged that Creuse isn't worth much, mycologically speaking) as well as berry- and root-based tinctures and liqueurs both medicinal and epicurean. I rarely stayed more than a day or two. Robert, the husband, possessed solid agricultural knowledge; he was a man of a practical turn of mind, but not devoid of subtlety or intelligence either. My mother could have done worse. I am in his debt for several good tips on the intensive silviculture of Vancouver fir trees, one of the best mushroom-producing conifers, along with the common spruce and the Scotch pine (a comprehensive knowledge of *Pinaceae* is absolutely crucial in life). I always chuckle when I see amateur mycologists combing forests of larch or Douglas fir in search of "brown gold" (i.e., the cep; I have great hopes that the metaphor will catch on). The Douglas is a tree unsuitable for any mycological purpose, whatever anyone may claim, and thus a worthless tree in general, but because it grows faster and seems more resistant to climatic vagaries than its competitors, it has over the last fifty years become the preferred conifer of more than one Corrèze landowner seduced by the prospect of optimal yield and accrued gain. It goes without saying that this is an appalling attitude. I advise you strongly not to plant Douglas firs, the parasite of the forests (see the attached photo of the enemy, easily recognizable by the often wispy look of its branches and its bottlebrush-like clusters of needles, which are curved and flexible, without marked white or bluish bands on the back).

I dare you to find a single Douglas fir on my land. Indeed, I have personally led resolute and systematic anti-Douglas campaigns for several years running in the village of Charlanne and the surrounding cantons. A carefully thought-out selection of plots of this undesirable conifer were subjected, on my initiative, to the American method of *controlled burning*, a controversial action that consists of setting fire only to certain, highly targeted areas and then containing this fire—that, at least, is the theory; it is still commonly used in the American national parks, with the mixed results of which we are all aware. Of course, there were some misgivings and rumblings of revolt in the case of my campaign. However, I found a way of getting the message across, and this practice had the considerable advantage of raising awareness among the more recalcitrant members of the community, and drawing their attention to the risks inherent in planting Douglas firs.

I have also installed, within a radius of fifteen or twenty kilometres around the château, measures aimed at protecting any wooded space in which ceps or girolles grow. This is to prevent nearby landowners from clearing or exploiting even the smallest cep breeding ground (they are strongly advised to avoid even passing through these areas between May and the end of November). Indeed, I do not believe the death penalty would be excessive for someone who cut down a cep forest. You might think of what I have done as establishing the very first mycological reserve. Naturally, I reserve the rights of both passage and harvest, but my intentions are scientific and aesthetic above all, you understand. And I consider myself the spiritual guardian of these lands; the fact that they have changed owners over the course of the past two centuries due to the ineptness of some ancestor or other does not affect this in the least.

I am no longer sure if I've already mentioned it, but I have drawn up a series of maps (1/2000 and 1/200 scale for the most fertile parcels) indicating the cep population by year, season, and forest type. Beyond their obvious usefulness, these maps, painted in oil in well-chosen hues of brown, green, and deep red, have an undeniable aesthetic value. Many is the time I have lost myself in contemplation of their spots and shadows, savouring the often-unexpected intersection of points and wavy lines, even seeing animal or plant shapes no cloud-gazer could ever hope to equal. Mycological topography, conducted with scientific rigour and artistic sensibility (I am fortunate enough to possess both), is an interdisciplinary specialization that does not yet benefit from the recognition it deserves; it remains, shamefully, the great lacuna in academic research.

But I digress! I wonder if this tendency to tangential musings is due to my age or the fact that I have so many things preoccupying me. Indeed, I have so much on my mind at present that I feel I have become a bit scattered; it's time to pull myself together. *De me ressaisir*. When my sister makes her next attempt she will find me no easy mark, of *that* you can be sure. I must absolutely be in full possession of my faculties—that is one of the reasons why I eat so many Portuguese sardines (sardines are excellent for mental acuteness, you know). Even Grivaud, our unfortunate old family physician, used to sing the praises of sardines during the biannual medical examinations to which I was subjected for my entire childhood. "Nikonor, my young friend, eat your sardines; they'll make you smart," he used to bellow, with a self-satisfied boom of laughter. If Grivaud died at a great age, it was only because he had proven a valuable ally by virtue of his stunning incompetence. That saved his life. My motto is that it's always good to have a bad doctor handy. Anyway, he was right about the sardines.

Encore que . . . suddenly I am seized with doubt! Perhaps it's one of those ridiculous old wives' tales, passed down from generation to generation, with a certain authority conferred by the years, but in fact lacking any scientific basis. God knows. It is so difficult sometimes to tell truth from falsehood . . . especially when one lacks an Internet connection. It's so easy to do a bit of research these days; no need to weigh oneself down with all those encyclopaedias in umpteen volumes. I've been thinking of giving the château's library a good spring cleaning; must get to that as soon as possible. Except that, as I said, I don't have the Internet here, so I can't check about the sardines . . . but enough whining; they can wait—and besides, I have too many tins stored up to suddenly stop eating them now. And really, after all, they've served me pretty well so far . . .

So, as I was saying, my stepfather was a pleasant enough man, with whom I always enjoyed chatting for a few moments about this or that. His ownership of La Jeaunerie, a huge farm complex whose main house dated from the seventeenth century, had a certain rustic charm as well. The room they gave me when I visited, with its immense carved wardrobe and its ancient cherry-wood bed (the box-spring rather dilapidated, it's true) was rather pleasant, except for its view—Robert parked his tractors just beneath my window. The surrounding landscape left much to be desired, however. The gentle green countryside lacked conifers, which is the case in much of Creuse, and I used to become quite lost in thought at the vision of such rural desolation each night before I closed my shutters. How on earth had my mother come to be in this place? How had she been able to trade the romantic wooded heights of Dordogne for this dull rustic life which, by the look of things, was hardly doing her any favours?

Indeed, during my last visit home, I found my mother both older-looking and heavier than I remembered her. Her once-celebrated beauty had been erased, had vanished completely, over the preceding year. She seemed distant and preoccupied, and didn't even think to ask me about my law firm in Paris. I have an image in my mind, now, of her as I was leaving. I had just managed, with great difficulty, to start my father's old DS (already temperamental) and was ready to leave their property and head for the connecting road. I turned around to salute her. She stood as if frozen on the front steps, face turned in profile, looking astonishingly like the portraits of Madame Manet. It was that moment, that melancholy snapshot, that fixed my mother's features in my memory forever.

※

I insisted that they be buried together in Creuse. The cemetery at La Charlanne was no Père-Lachaise in its capaciousness, and after all, my mother was reaping what she had sown. She would have to bear responsibility for her own choices to the end. Besides, one of their neighbours, no doubt invited at the last moment to share their dinner of Correzian delicacies, had met the same sad fate, so Ahun's funeral parlours were enjoying a run of good luck; it would hardly have done to hurt their business by stealing two-thirds of their clientele. It might even have stirred up old rivalries between Creuse and Corrèze, which would have been unacceptable. I am, and have always been, a firm partisan of interdepartmental peace.[1]

✳

The funeral was a well-executed affair. Because Robert, my stepfather, was a firm atheist, we dispensed with the usual mass. There must have been nearly a hundred of us in the cemetery at Ahun, there to accompany the three corpses to their final reward (it had been decided to proceed with a group burial in order to maximize the funerary impact on a local population always on the lookout for this type of windfall). Uniform, gravel-covered grey paths separated rows of pink or grey marble and granite tombstones adorned with wreaths of artificial flowers discoloured by wind and rain, along with plaques containing phrases such as "To my beloved aunt" and "To our dear neighbour with fond remembrances".

Not an ounce of greenery to be seen in any direction. French cemeteries are generally depressing, stomach-turning places. They tend to make me seasick. If you're craving an especially acute bout of nausea, be sure not to miss the cemetery at Limoges, which is second to none in the "supermarket of death" category. I think these places are designed above all as a severe warning to non-believers: *Beware, infidels; if you don't believe in heaven and the great beyond, this is where you will end up, in this grey and forbidding no man's land.* I greatly prefer English and Russian cemeteries, which

1 With the exception of a brief phase devoted to Correzian separatism, which I shall blame on the foolishness of youth.

are always green and welcoming, with a pastoral ambiance conducive to daydreaming. A much more satisfactory final resting place than these endless grey stretches. The family necropolis at La Charlanne, with its wild grasses, its stone crosses weathered by time, its romantic atmosphere, is also an altogether more attractive place than the Ahun cemetery.

Up to the very last moment, I wondered if Anastasie would have the gall to make an appearance. I watched for her during every minute of the event; I would not have missed her entrance. Once I even thought I recognized her, bundled up in an old-ladyish flowered shawl, but further investigation proved beyond a doubt that this was, in fact, a distant cousin of Robert's from Auvergne—a *divorcée*, they made sure to tell me, in disapproval-tinged voices.

The relatives of the collateral victim put on quite a show of weeping and wailing (one might have thought oneself in the middle of a Greek tragedy), which spoiled the otherwise restrained and dignified atmosphere of the ceremony. Vaguely nauseated, I decided not to stick around Ahun and as soon as was seemly I made for my DS, which I'd parked in front of the war memorial in the town square. As I passed, I noted with approval that Robert's family was very well-represented among the Sons of Ahun who had given their lives for the Motherland. That was something, at least. Poor Robert certainly couldn't boast of such service, himself. As a nameless victim of *Cortinarius speciosissimus*, or deadly webcap (a member of the genus *Cortinarius* which appears mainly in late summer and autumn, largely in conifer woods; it grows particularly well near the spruce in humid areas, often with peaty soil, where—I must admit—I often have great difficulty locating it), he had now been deprived of the opportunity to leave his mark in the family annals once and for all. But we mustn't exaggerate, either; there was nothing about Robert that suggested he might be capable of having a lasting effect on the planet, and besides, after all, no one had asked him to marry my mother. No one had forced him to do it. He'd wanted a *châtelaine anglaise*, and he'd gotten one. Now he could bloody well lie in the bed he'd made. Perhaps my father was enjoying the spectacle, from beyond the grave. One hoped so, at least.

Before leaving, I'd asked Robert's only son, one Jean, a mousy little fellow[1] whose features I can no longer remember, for permission to take a few things from the house that had belonged to my mother. My request was granted with good grace. It may also help you a bit in the way of background to know that I had informed Jean of my intention to renounce any share in the inheritance from the Creuse estate, a piece of information that was extremely well-received.

What had he expected me to say? I wanted nothing to do with any of that. The lure of financial gain had never entered into my decision-making process, and now I could return to Corrèze with my head held high.

When I reached the farmhouse, I went straight to the room my mother had shared with her second husband. I hoped to find a letter, a private diary, anything that would give me some indication of Anastasie's

---

1 How I adore that word, "mousy", straight out of a crime novel. Any detective story worth its salt has a *mousy* character in it somewhere.

whereabouts, and—even more importantly—of how she had managed to turn my mother against me. Because she most certainly had. I had realized it the minute I saw how morose and distracted my mother was. Anastasie was behind it. She had planted a seed of doubt; she had sowed discord between mother and son. It was pathetic—but, alas, wholly typical of the way she operated.

I just needed to know how she had done it, and exactly what rubbish she had spewed about me. I could trust no one.

I searched every piece of furniture in the room thoroughly (a bureau/wardrobe/bed/nightstand set in heavy walnut, modern and garish; my mother must have had no say whatsoever in the decoration of the house) but found nothing conclusive. Only bills for jewellery, two prescriptions for blood-pressure medication, and a long letter from Marie, several years old already, which I read carefully several times without discovering anything even remotely suspicious in it. But I decided to take it with me just in case, to read again later, when I could give it my full attention. One never knew; it could be an *hareng rouge* planted by Anastasie to mislead the enemy.

I have just reread that last sentence, and it strikes me that it might be quite nonsensical to someone unfamiliar with the English expression "red herring", which my subconscious (if there is such a thing) has taken the liberty of translating literally—the French language must be capable of absorbing a few literal translations now and again, after all; otherwise, what is to become of us? This is an expression roughly equivalent to the French stock phrase *fausse piste*, or *wrong track* (*to go*

110

down the wrong track, etc.). Its origins are said to lie in an old English technique for training hunting dogs in which a herring, smoked to the point of acquiring a vivid red-brown hue, was dangled in front of a young dog. The intention of this was to teach it to distinguish the scent of its true prey (foxes, badgers, etc.) from the strong odour of the herring—an admirably imaginative method. However, some linguists contest the validity of this colourful etymological explanation, deeming it nebulous (or even *fishy*, as it were) and probably erroneous—all of which is distinctly ironic, as I'm sure you will agree. This *red herring*, by the by, has nothing at all to do with Charles Cros's famous *hareng saur*, or smoked herring, immortalised in the poem of the same name thus: *Il était un grand mur blanc / nu, nu, nu, / Contre le mur une échelle / haute, haute, haute, /Et, par terre, un hareng saur / sec, sec, sec.*[1] Do not confuse the two.

Whatever. *Hareng rouge* or *hareng saur*, I had to face reality: my sister Anastasie had vanished into thin air. *Volatilisée.*

I couldn't have imagined, back then, that I would have to wait more than half a century before she resurfaced.

---

1 *Once upon a time there was a high white wall / bare, bare, bare, / Against this wall there stood a ladder / high, high, high, / And, on the ground, a smoked herring/ dry, dry, dry.*

8

Le compte à rebours, the final countdown, is close at hand now, though I can't say if it will be tomorrow or if it is weeks away yet—nor can I tell exactly how events will play out. Whatever happens, I am ready. Things are no longer dependent on me, and I accept without complaint the role of passive, introspective spectator which circumstances have now assigned to me. Though my nights are becoming more and more restless, full of bizarre, exhausting dreams, my daily life is a well-oiled machine, with my little habits ever more entrenched. I no longer occupy the blue bedroom of my boyhood, which needs a great deal of work—violent rains have damaged the delicate *toile de Jouy* wallpaper my mother chose after I had left for Paris; there is a deep crack across a whole section of one wall. I wake up at dawn, drenched in sweat, in the huge metal-framed bed in our old guest room. The fire is always long dead by then, and the air is glacial. To get to the bathrooms, you have to go down to the kitchen and through a long, stone-paved corridor. The kitchen door is always half-open, and every morning I glimpse the same bit of frieze—grapes, painted in the nineteen-twenties. That frieze is my chime of memory, my *madeleine*, my sugared violet—the sight that defined my childhood—and snippets of the past spring to my mind with the regularity of the old clock in the library. How many hours of my life have I spent in that kitchen, helping with the mysterious alchemical process that is the preparation of a meal, or sitting on a bench at the enormous wooden table, back to the stove, eating my snack of brown bread with jam on a winter's afternoon? My eyes never failed to light on that frieze, to count and recount obsessively the number of individual grapes in each purple bunch (fifteen in total, of which nine are entirely visible), interspersed with broad vine leaves, and then the number of bunches around the whole upper perimeter of the kitchen: 150, or ten times the number of grapes. Without really knowing how to interpret the thought, I saw in those harmonic numbers the cabalistic sign of a higher order. Now that morning glance at the bunches of grapes invariably sends me into a gently wistful reverie. Who knows, perhaps my life would have gone in a different direction without that viticultural frieze, to which I owe my ability to concentrate, my discipline of mind.

The indignities to which many people fall prey at my advanced age have spared me, happily. My overall health is robust and I have a stomach of cast iron, unperturbed even by the cheesy excesses of a *truffade*. I am still tall, straight-backed and neat, and though my face has lost the patrician perfection of my youth, my eyes retain the bright blue sparkle that has won me a perhaps unreasonable number of conquests over the years.

For the first time in my life, I am feeling the urge to unburden myself, to explain my choices and my personal tastes. I wouldn't even be averse to the idea of writing out one of those bucket lists—"Ten things to do, books to read, or places to visit before you die." Of course, I would carefully avoid the nonsense answers you find all over women's magazines —of which, by the way, I have become a devoted reader since coming to the château. I never forget to buy the latest issue of *Femme actuelle*, *Elle*, or *Marie-Claire* when I go into Mauriac, in part because it's important to get inside the enemy's mind. These magazines give me precious insight into Anastasie's way of thinking, which helps me maintain the competitive advantage. None of that "take a cruise around the world" (my personal vision of hell) or "swim with dolphins" foolishness: the nasty things bite. The dolphin is one of those animals that infects people with a sort of "Disney syndrome"; every year, adults, as well as children hop into the water with perfect confidence, all ready to stroke those pretty, cuddly creatures, which are quite ready to rip off an arm or a leg (I'm not speaking exclusively of cetaceans now, as you might have guessed) . . .

"Take a trip to a Caribbean island paradise" is another recurring (and nauseating) wish common among our degenerate Western societies, or perhaps, more fairly (and optimistically), among their mutual lowest common denominator. This can never be said often enough: "island paradise" is an oxymoron; all islands are, by definition, vile places, geographic pustules that disfigure the oceans—especially if they are "exotic", meaning full of palm trees (a ridiculous tree; unsightly, coarse, and mycologically useless), ringed by fine sand beaches, and afflicted with a sunny climate. We should all be fighting furiously against this particularly durable cliché with its determination to impose an island vision of paradise, which is found wholesale (the cliché, I mean) in Plato, Ovid, Lucian of Samosata, countless travel agency brochures, and even the Venerable Bede of Northumbria, who disgraced himself in the eighth century by contributing to the implantation of the "island paradise" myth in the collective imagination.

Paradisiacal cartography is a fascinating discipline; I am not disputing that. But the sunny regions are infinitely overrepresented in it, to my way of thinking. For my part, I tend to place paradise resolutely in the North. I cannot claim that my theory is supported by any mythological or theological crutch; it is simply intuition, the sort of warming flash of certainty I have experienced so often in my life. More precisely, the heavenly landscape is one of birches, aspens and conifers (with a glimpse of tundra in the background, perhaps), interwoven with sparkling rivers filled with wriggling trout and salmon. Though markedly different from this automatic description (in the surrealist sense of the word), the most convincing visual representation I know of is the Norwegian artist Nikolai Astrup's painting, *Girls in the Woods*. Notice, however, that Astrup did not dare to use the word "paradise" in reference to this work; the poor man, he must have feared the repercussions—accusations of sacrilege, or even a proper Scandinavian witch-hunt.

Upon further reflection, and to facilitate the work of those who will have the daunting task of ensuring my legacy, I have decided to fill out Proust's famous questionnaire. I do not intend to be taken for an enigmatic *poseur* who keeps the flame of his own legend by refusing to reveal anything about himself.

Here it is. NB: I have taken the liberty of disregarding the silly first question, and have permitted myself a few liberties of principle here and there, but the essence of the questionnaire has, I believe, been respected.

The principal aspect of my personality:

I prefer to use the English word here: *resilience*. The ability to adapt to my environment, like any predator worthy of the name.

My favourite qualities in a man:

Erudition. And men who can be quiet and *take the rap*, again as the English say. The strong, silent type.

My favourite qualities in a woman:

Faithfulness and decency. I'd also like to make it clear that I am not a misogynist *per se*.

My main fault:

Because I have an artist's temperament at heart (in the sense that the term was used by good old Edmond de Goncourt), I have an occasional tendency to indulge in improvisation; to give free rein to a certain poetic licence, a fantasy of performance which, in hindsight, is sometimes misleading.

My chief characteristic:

Intelligence and strength of character, which complement one another perfectly within me.

What I appreciate most about my friends:

I have very few friends (or "had", I should say, since the individuals in question are all dead at present); I am not very "sociable" by nature. But, to answer the question, let me say that when a fragile bond of mutual esteem and respect *has* been established, I enjoy being the expert advisor to my friends for any question having to do with mycology. I appreciate the fact that they consume the mushrooms I recommend or give to them without hesitation. For me, this is a lovely proof of friendship, and one which, *au bout de compte*, I have abused only rarely.

My favourite occupation:

I think I have already provided a clear answer to this question: looking for ceps in a beautiful forest, preferably a mossy one. I have no objection to the presence of underbrush, low branches, fallen tree-trunks, tall grass, brambles, shrubs, broom, or heather—all obstacles and hiding places that make the quest for the capricious cep as exciting as a big-game hunt in Africa, with all due respect to Hemingway. I am quite a bit less enthusiastic about the idea of being luncheon for a tick, as they are likely to carry Lyme disease, a bacterial illness that can certainly be treated with enormous doses of antibiotics, but rarely before transforming you into a vegetable for months. One must be able to live dangerously in order to be worthy of the cep. Though inoffensive to walkers, the large, bright orange slugs that abound in the Correzian undergrowth constitute another type of harmful vermin, which attack the cep relentlessly and, through their voracious snacking, sometimes alter its sublime beauty.

But, enough discussion.

You are walking through damp underbrush on a crisp autumn morning. The thick carpet of leaves and needles crackles beneath your feet; a small breeze rustles the highest branches of this green cathedral. You are alone[1], far from everything, and you breathe in the heady scent of decomposing plant matter and pine sap. You are on the lookout, every sense alert, when, suddenly, your heart beats faster. You have just seen this (see photo below; I am particularly proud of that one, taken in an undisclosed location on a cloudless summer afternoon).

A small miracle has occurred. In an instant it has become possible to capture the essence of beauty, the Holy Grail of the forest. A well-conducted cep-hunting expedition can become a mystical experience (especially in the absence of mosquitoes). Sometimes a single discovery can turn into an unexpected mother lode, and you no longer know even where to look, because that is not one, but three, five, ten, twenty mischievous caps that you have just spotted; a long rosary of forest Buddhas, ready to participate in some mysterious sylvan ritual. My personal record is 42 ceps within a single area of a few square meters. Not

---

1 I would advise you strongly against searching for ceps with a companion. My sister, who frequently invited herself along with complete shamelessness on my cep-hunting expeditions, chattered incessantly on any number of bizarre and ridiculous subjects, disturbing the fragile quiet of the forest. Notoriously incapable of finding the cep, even with precise directions, more than once she even *stepped on* the specimens I was attempting to help her discover. My earliest fratricidal thoughts date back to that part of my childhood.

every cep incurs the same aesthetic appreciation; the most beautiful ones have a wide round stem topped with a deep red, almost violet cap (the tubes and pores should be white, of course, which is a sign of freshness, though some yellow-pored specimens can be solid and pleasing to the eye. Large ceps covered with green "moss", when robust, also have a certain charm, as do the plump little ceps known by the charming sobriquet *bouchon de champagne*, or champagne corks. Squat, red-violet pine ceps, known as *têtes de nègre*, or Negro's heads (I do not keep up with the tribulations of political correctness, and am therefore not in a position to offer you a substitute designation), are relatively rare—but, in ceps and in gems, rarity only increases desirability.

My idea of happiness:

What is happiness? An enormous question indeed, one which philosophers and baccalaureate candidates have mulled over for centuries (in the case of the former, at least, since the baccalaureate was only introduced in 1808 by Napoleon I, and I doubt very much that the first candidates would have given this type of question a great deal of thought; they probably would have deemed it pointless). Personally, I reject any definition that imposes rigid moral or ethical constraints (*oui*, I'm looking at you, Spinoza and Kant) or half-measures (the term "satisfaction", of either the senses or the psyche, should be strictly banned). Happiness is a state of absolute fulfilment, which has nothing to do with morality. It is difficult to attain—without resorting to illicit substances, that is—and even harder to maintain long-term. It goes without saying that "love"

119

is an illusion in which most people choose to remain stubbornly entangled; unfortunately, I cannot claim to be an exception in that regard.

But I have learnt my lesson.

In view of my venerable age, I believe I am within my rights to bestow on you a few tips and tricks. Two absolutely essential conditions must be met simultaneously, if you aspire to a dose of "happiness": nature and solitude. Fear not; I am not going to bombard you with a remix of Thoreau or Rousseau, but I do have a personal ideal situation in mind: a log cabin (fully furnished and equipped with all the modern comforts and a large fireplace—I am a hermit, not an ascetic) in Colorado, or Alaska, or perhaps Siberia. I can also see myself at Nikko, in Japan, in a stone temple in the middle of a thousand-year-old emerald-green forest. Failing those, La Charlanne suits me perfectly, though, because there I can explore the mysteries of mycology to my heart's content.

What would be my greatest unhappiness?
It has already happened.

If not myself, who would I be?
    . . .

Where would I like to live?
See "my idea of happiness".

My favourite colour:
Our Monsieur Proust acts like a teenage girl sometimes, no? My favourite colour is, without a doubt, crimson. Carmine red. Burgundy. Garnet. Claret.

(NB: I have skipped completely over the next two questions about flowers and birds. I am not in a playful mood.)

My favourite prose writers:

Finally, a subject worth stopping on. But, so as not to show off my degree of learning, which might alienate a twenty-first-century readership, I will limit myself to a single answer to this monumental question (for which I hope Nabokov, Paul Bowles, Hemingway, and many others will forgive me): Michel Houellebecq. Detesting Houellebecq today makes about as much sense as hating Baudelaire or Zola in the nineteenth century. It places you squarely in the losers' camp, along with Ernest Pinard, the attorney who prosecuted both *Madame Bovary* and Baudelaire with immortal oratory such as the following:

> "I say, gentlemen, that lascivious detail cannot be compensated for by a moral conclusion; otherwise one could describe every possible type of orgy, enumerate all the depravities of a prostitute, by having her die on a pallet in a hospital. In this way it would be permissible to dwell on, to show, every one of her lascivious acts! Such an attitude would go against every rule of good sense. It would be to place poison within easy reach of everyone, and the antidote within reach of only a few—if such an antidote even existed. Who is reading Monsieur Flaubert's nov-

121

el? Is it the men who attend to political or social economy? No! The flimsy pages of *Madame Bovary* are falling into far daintier hands; into the hands of young girls, and even married women."

As you see. Utter prudish losers destined to be sneered at by future generations in critical editions of *les classiques de la littérature française* (that is, if this type of book is to live on, and I wouldn't bank on it). It is turgid, bombastic rhetoric, every piece of it virtually identical. Houellebecq, according to his anachronistic detractors, writes "putrid literature" (the same accusation made in 1868 against Zola and Naturalism) without style. Desperate times!

As I have aged, I have also realized that some authors I used to adore have suddenly become too overwrought for my nervous system. I am thinking in particular of the Russians; Dostoyevsky certainly, and Tolstoy to a lesser extent. Nor can I stomach Chateaubriand any longer; he is too much of a crybaby. On the other hand, I find Gogol much more pleasing now.

My favourite poets:
Poetry, in the modern era, is a worthless and obsolete genre deserving of nothing more than to be classified as a vintage curiosity.

My favourite heroes in fiction:
John Lanchester's Tarquin Winot possesses a certain panache, in spite of his limited mycological knowledge. I also enjoy most of the characters in the novels

of Houellebecq and Haruki Murakami. Otherwise, Meursault has always delighted me; he is priceless. In my humble opinion, he is one of the greatest comic creations in French literature, and my stomach often hurts from laughing when I reread *L'Étranger*.

My favourite heroines in fiction:
Hmm . . . Thérèse Desqueyroux. Even though she failed, regrettably, in her attempt at conjugal poisoning. In the end, even in a fictional context, this goes back to one of my earlier observations: it is important, even essential, to have access to an idiotic family doctor, who never notices anything and will mistake the symptoms of orellanine ingestion for gastric upset.

My favourite composers:
I only listen to classic rock. My favourite song: *Stairway to Heaven*.

My favourite painters:
Paolo Uccello (those hunting scenes in forests). Astrup. Sánchez Cotan. For tapestry, I adore "Les Chasses de Maximilien", particularly the wild boar hunt set in December. I also have a weakness for medieval art—the "Très Riches Heures du duc de Berry", and the Labours of the Months at Buonconsiglio Castle in Trento; the month of April especially, in which you can see fresh little white mushrooms on the edge of a dark forest. Except for the fact that, of course, this kind of mushroom wouldn't grow in April; morels should have been put in instead—but I can't really criticise a medieval artist for these errors; he might have been obeying the whims of a moronic patron.

My favourite heroines in real life:

My mother. Before she went over to the enemy. Before her defection, as inexplicable as it was cruel.

My historical heroes:

It will not have escaped your attention, I'm sure, that the idea of a "hero" is highly random, representing an idea terrifying in its fluidity. The worst villains in history are often the subject of cultish worship, just like the heroes. Moreover, a man who is a hero in one era may well be seen as a traitor or villain in the next, or vice versa. See, for example, the pathetic fate of Pétain, who simply didn't know when to die. I have been mulling over this scenario for some time. I hope, for my own part, that I will know to take my final bow when the moment is right. As in every situation in life, one must know how to act with class and elegance. There is nothing worse than a guest who has overstayed his welcome.

My absolute favourite historical hero is Ivan IV of Russia, known as Ivan the Terrible, mainly for his untameable spirit, his panache, his sense of colour. It was he who built the onion-domed marvel that is Saint Basil's Cathedral, in commemoration of the capture of Kazan, the capital of the Tatars, by the Russians in 1552. According to legend, Ivan then had the architects' eyes gouged out so that they could never create another such magnificent building—an overly zealous interpretation of copyright law or the Intellectual Property Code, perhaps, but after all, it was sixteenth-century Russia, and Ivan IV never troubled himself much with legal concerns. Vlad IV of Wallachia (nicknamed Vlad the Impaler) wasn't too bad himself, for that matter. Their stories were delicious fun when I was a boy, and they were certainly more colourful than the dull ogres that peopled traditional fairy tales.

My favourite things to eat and drink:

I am the victim of a singularly bad joke on the part of the higher power, if it exists (a claim of which I have no proof, nor do I particularly want any). Though my love of the forest world is absolute, as you will have been able to tell by now even if you have only a shred of intelligence or an average attention span, I have very little appetite for its "fruits" — by which I mean berries, game animals, and — O, cruel irony! — mushrooms. I, who have elevated the cep to an object of aesthetic worship, am incapable of appreciating its subtle flavour! But I believe I have resolved this apparent paradox: if one of my first and primary mycological motivations had been the pure, simple, and prosaic consumption of the cep, my aesthetic appreciation of it would have been dulled considerably. *Quod erat demonstrandum.* On the other hand, and I suppose there is a sort of profound equilibrium, a harmony, a symmetry in all of this, to answer the Proustian question and avoid any further delay liable to lose the interest of my readership, I will confess an immoderate weakness for seafood: oysters, scallops, langoustines, prawns, whelks, crabs. Despite my pronounced — and fully justified — dislike of seas, beaches, swimming, and other aquatic horrors, I have often gone all the way to Landes or Bretagne for the simple pleasure of a seafood dinner. The ideal accompaniment would be a 1966 Bienvenues-Bâtard-Montrachet, or perhaps a

1971. There; I have answered the question. I am not doing too badly, it seems to me; I flatter myself that I am even beginning to excel at this interview game. Perhaps there is a star lurking behind this gruff hermit's face . . .

What I hate the most:
Fear. I don't believe I have ever felt that contemptible emotion, though it is apparently commonplace and inherent in human nature. It is important not to confuse fear with that tension of all the senses, that rush of adrenaline, that feeling of urgency experienced by the predator ready to unloose every muscle in a lightning-quick attack that must necessarily be fatal to one of the parties involved. However, I did once feel a sort of latent discomfort, an insidious unease which, if it had lasted more than a few weeks, would eventually have weakened my habitual self-control.

Catastrophe was narrowly avoided, that time. If it will entertain you, I will recount the circumstances.

Two residents of the area around La Charlanne had gone missing under strange circumstances, five weeks apart. According to their families, they had vanished into thin air in a completely inexplicable and disturbing way. Monsieur Vallet had gone out to look for ceps on a bright, cool morning in late October. He had gotten up at sunrise and drunk a quick cup of coffee; his wife had heard the car rumble away from the house and gone back to sleep. The Taillandot boy's situation was a bit less clear, as his mother's version of events differed from his grandmother's. He had announced his intention to go and look for chestnuts on the wooded hills overlooking the Dordogne gorges (his mother's

126

recollection)—or perhaps it was apples he was looking for, on the family land along the Ussel road (the grandmother's story, slightly less credible given the deafness of the lady in question). Vallet's basket had been found in a beech grove a few kilometres outside the village and his red car parked two hundred metres away from that, undoubtedly in an attempt to prevent any mushroom-hunters from discovering the nearby patch of ceps (not a very productive one, between you and me). The man could not have suspected that, less than one hundred metres away, in a thicket of underbrush, lay a lode of top-quality girolles. Taillandot had left no visible trace, and his whereabouts were still the subject of intense investigative speculation. After the second disappearance, a major police enquiry had been launched. A well-respected inspector from the Toulouse crime squad had been dispatched to the area (I forget his name . . . Verlugnac? Berluac? A stunted little man, anyway, with a mournful expression and a Groucho Marx moustache). At his instigation, sinister connections had been made to the disappearance of that old bastard Legrandin—or "that louse Legrandin", as my mother used to say; like many non-native French speakers, she had an ear for alliteration—more than a decade earlier, and to the case of a gamekeeper who had gone missing during a forest ramble and been assumed at the time simply to have run away.

Nothing good could come of the business. There was even talk of searching wells and bodies of water in the region; frogmen had already explored a whole section of the Dordogne, from its junction with the Sumène river to the Saint-Projet bridge. For two full weeks, considerable agitation had reigned over the area. Police vans careered at full tilt over roads and paths not really made for that sort of traffic. The place crawled with people, like an enormous anthill. The local rags speculated with their usual relish about the existence of a *tueur en série* ("Le 'Pays vert': last refuge of a serial killer?"; "Mysterious disappearances of mushroom-hunters: is a serial killer at work in the forests of Corrèze?"; etc.), while rumours of every kind flew hither and yon among the surrounding villages; i.e., Monsieur Vallet, the owner of the abandoned basket, who enjoyed—rightly or wrongly (I refuse to engage in that sort of small-town gossip)—a reputation as a bit of a horny devil, had been spotted in the company of a pretty blonde and/or brunette in Tulle and/or Rocadamour. And the mother and grandmother of the Taillandot lad, who were daughter-in-law and mother-in-law, to be exact, were no longer speaking except to fling sordid, Maupassantesque accusations of inheritance, adultery, and incest at one another. Et cetera.

Several intensive searches of the countryside had been carried out, and I casually joined one of them. As a good lord of the manor, I had even provided refreshments for all the participants at the end of the day. The drawing room, tidied up for the occasion, looked impressive indeed; the immense *bois-des-îles* table, covered with one of my paternal grandmother's linen cloths, held a substantial repast: meat pies, trays of charcuterie and cheeses, apple *clafoutis*; even carafes of a quite passable *petit Bordeaux*. All very correct. The occasion provided me with the opportunity of exchanging friendly small talk with Inspector Vergnouc (... or, was it Berlac? No—I think it was Borland), who turned out to be a cultivated fellow, with whom it was quite possible to have a reasonably stimulating conversation.

I showed him around the library. Passionately fond of military history, he went into raptures over my original edition of *Idées d'un militaire pour la disposition des troupes* (1783) by Charles Louis François Fossé. Leafing through the pages of the book with infinite delicacy—even excessive, but endearing—he emitted exclamations of enthusiasm of which I hadn't thought him capable when I'd first met him. When he left, I accompanied him personally to the gates of the château, where we parted on the most amicable terms. He had offered his condolences on my recent losses— my mother and stepfather—and revealed that he was quite worried about his own mother, who often failed to recognize him and had tried to seduce one of the young doctors assigned to her care. Moreover, the investigation was going nowhere; the work promised to be of long duration, and he wasn't yet ready to return to Toulouse. He went so far as to confide in me that they currently had no leads whatsoever, that the situation was exhausting in every sense. They could only hope for a breakthrough, a witness, or a body, as soon as possible, he sighed.

I learned several lessons from this regrettable business: *primo*, it was time, as a matter of urgency, to restock the fishpond with carp (I would also get a dozen pike, in case they might be of use); and, *secundo*, I would have to avoid at all costs any further interaction, no matter how cordial and civilized, with the local, regional, national, or international law enforcement. With this in mind, I decided that it would be ill-advised to continue to participate in personal "clean-up" operations here, or in the surrounding areas. The elimination of an associate with paranoid tendencies that became necessary a year or two later was an exception to this rule, but the operation was carried out with the greatest discretion and did not arouse the slightest suspicion. No one ever even knew, as far as I am aware, that he had made the trip from Paris to La Charlanne by car, and ended up as fertilizer for the pumpkins in the château's garden.

Where was I?

This Proustian questionnaire is becoming tedious, so I shall wrap it up quickly. The weather is particularly cold today, and I have had to leave off writing every five or ten minutes to tend to the fire. I am also drinking copious amounts of herbal tea in order to warm up, and with the resultant diuretic consequences I am having some difficulty concentrating.

My least favourite historical figure:

Without feeling any actual animosity or resentment towards him, I find Jesus of Nazareth to occupy an excessive place in history. I have little appreciation for characters who invite themselves onto the historical scene for a period of several centuries like that. *Ne vous y trompez pas*; he is one of the greatest attention-seekers (*mais . . . comment dit-on en français?*) of all time (it is fortunate that this isn't the nineteenth century, or I would quickly be hauled into court on a charge of "moral and religious indecency"). On the other hand—and I refuse to see anything contradictory in this—I have a great attachment to churches, monasteries, and places of worship of every type, with their atmosphere of meditation and silence. A contemplative life in a cell, a life of reading, of walks in the forest and the mountains, would have suited me very well. At one time I even considered retiring to the Grande Chartreuse monastery in Isère. A formal request had been duly submitted to the appropriate authorities, but after a lengthy and gruelling series of formalities, I received a letter informing me that my Carthusian spirituality had been deemed insufficient. It was not meant to happen. *C'est la vie.*

My least favourite historical events:

Oh, there are plenty of these! But the sale of Alaska to America in 1867 easily wins the prize, followed closely by the Belgian colonization of the Congo (on this subject, allow me to recommend the eye-opening *Le Congo: à quoi il doit nous servir, ce que nous devons y faire, conférence par M. Charles Morisseaux, ingénieur honoraire des Mines, directeur général du secrétariat au ministère de l'Industrie et du Travail, membre du Conseil colonial* (Brussels, printed by A. Lesigne, 1911).

The military exploit I admire the most:

I do not hold soldiers in any particular esteem, no matter their beliefs, and should certainly not be counted on to stroke their virile egos.

The reform I admire the most:

Though I am not overtly reactionary, I am no reformist either, which has not prevented me from embracing modernity; I am known for delighting in new technological gadgets, and the fact that my mobile telephone does not work at La Charlanne is a source of great irritation. My conservatism is exclusively socio-political in nature.

The natural ability I would most like to possess:

The gift of clairvoyance, obviously.

The way in which I would like to die:

I would be lying if I said the question had not crossed my mind over the past few weeks. My answer: free.

My current state of mind:

Not too bad, *merci beaucoup*.

The fault I view most indulgently:

Avarice. A stingy old man huddled over his pile of gold coins always touches my heart (though I do not know anyone like that personally). The literary *topos* deserves to be revisited in depth, in order to give avarice its proper share of attention.

Who would you like to kill? What method would you use?

Tell me who you want to kill, and I will tell you who you are, or words to that effect. My answer to the first question is blindingly clear and dazzlingly simple, like everything that is beautiful, profound, and true in this world: Anastasie. I reserve the right not to answer the second question. I never swore to tell "the truth, the whole truth, and nothing but the truth", and I will leave it to you to separate fact and fiction, random and treacherous concepts that they are. As Hobbes so aptly observed (though he also wrote a great deal of nonsense), "truth and falsehood are attributes of speech, not of things. And where speech is not, there is neither truth nor falsehood." Still, that kind of interpretive quest is not to be undertaken lightly, and what you find out might devastate you. There; you have been warned. Let it never be said that I stabbed you in the back.

9

The moment has come. The sign I have been watching for day after day without knowing what form it would take appeared late this morning. The enemy has at last emerged from the shadows, has made the first move in this life-and-death chess game, and in a way, it's a relief for me. The man, disguised as a postman, must have been sent ahead by Anastasie as a scout. She has never hesitated to sacrifice pawns; it is part of her strategy. I recognize her personal touch. She is a coward, deep down. She would never have showed up herself for this final confrontation, this ultimate fraternal duel, though it would have fulfilled the theatrical concept of unity of place, found in Greek tragedy, almost perfectly: having arrived at the château together a century ago in a flow of amniotic fluid, we would now have mingled our blood and left it together, as well. Somewhat vulgar and overly romantic, I grant you, but the circle would at least have been completed: *order, symmetry, poetic justice.* Such a Hollywoodesque *grand finale* would have rocked, you must agree. Speaking strictly for myself, it would have been an acceptable resolution, though I sense that we are moving painfully toward a more Scandinavian noir-type ending. She has willed it thus.

Though constantly on the alert, I was nearly caught unawares by the pseudo-postman. I had just returned from the bathroom and was heading for the lounge, where I had spent part of the morning at my desk, re-transcribing my chicken-scratch into the Clairefontaine notebook. Three violent strikes of the door-knocker sounded at the entrance, accompanied by a loud cry of "Postman! Anyone home?" I gathered my wits quickly. It was too late to get the rifle, which I had forgotten on the kitchen table; my usual sharpness must have been dulled by a large breakfast of tea, scrambled eggs, yoghurt, and toast with honey, I suppose. A quick glance out an upper window told me that the lure was alone, or appeared to be, at least. He had apparently managed to avoid the fox-traps I had placed at regular intervals along the main embankment and all around the castle, which proved that he hadn't wasted any time searching on the road, but had come straight to the target. That was an interesting choice in itself. If I could get him inside, I might have a chance of overcoming him, which would give me the breathing space I needed to think about what to do next. I seized the fireplace poker with grim determination and went to open the door.

I believe I can say with confidence that my hand did not tremble, though I haven't had much practice in recent years. He seemed to suspect nothing until his fate was already sealed. Perhaps the apparent lack of wariness was part of his postman's act, but I rather think that my sister and her cronies had not told him how dangerous the consequences of his regrettable masquerade could be. Still, I must admit that it was a relatively successful performance; after all, who pays attention to the peregrinations of an inoffensive mail carrier in his canary-yellow minivan trundling along the back-country roads? His disguise was impeccable on every point: cap, blue-grey uniform with yellow trim, leather bag bulging with properly-stamped letters and newspapers addressed to residents of the area— with an unexpected, original touch here and there to reinforce the authenticity of the charade—I am thinking in particular of the letter from Bolivia supposedly intended for old lady Minesotti, and Monsieur Renart's delivery of silk stockings. My sister can be reproached for many things, but she is a perfectionist with an eye for detail. I decided to appropriate the contents of the mailbag, which would provide me with reading material for later. Neither did I discount the possibility that there might be a coded message for me somewhere, perhaps in one of the handwritten letters. In short, they had clearly spared no expense when it came to props and costumes, and an uninitiated person would not have been blamed for being fooled. A bit later I even discovered a yellow postal van parked sloppily in front of the château gates, which hardly surprised me at all. The only fault I could find with the deception was that they might even have carried it a bit too far; it seemed so "real" as to be almost a cliché.

The "postman" bled like a stuck pig all over the great stone slabs of the entryway floor, and I had to spend most of the day meticulously scrubbing them. I am no perfect housekeeper by any means, but I've been cleaning up after myself for more than fifty years and I am certainly a firm believer in the virtues of strict cleanliness and hygiene. They have saved my skin on more than one occasion. Of course, most of my career took place during the pre-DNA golden age. The profession has suffered a major blow in recent years, and its future prospects look gloomy indeed. It was with these melancholy thoughts coursing through my head that I transported the body in an old wheelbarrow into the barn, now transformed into a makeshift morgue. The yellow van was hidden from prying eyes in the capacious shed, which already houses the DS and two company cars. All of this required an effort that exhausted me; I was out of breath and had to sit down for a few moments to recover myself. I have gotten out of the habit of moving bodies. It is hardly a fit activity for a man of my age. As Jacques Laurent aptly put it, "old age is a foreign language that you have to learn at a time when the brain is no longer able to acquire new knowledge very easily."

But I cannot allow myself to rest on my laurels now. A mournful realisation has set in: I cannot remain at La Charlanne much longer. Other traps and lures will surely follow this one; I cherish no illusions about that; and they will only become more and more devious, more frequent, more unpredictable. And my sister and her henchmen will inevitably show up themselves, eventually. I have spent the evening crafting my strategy, a rather daring one: I have decided to withdraw permanently to the convent at La Thébaïde. As I believe I have already mentioned, La Thébaïde does not actually belong to me *d'un point de vue technique*, as much as it pains me to admit it. That solitary enclave is officially the property of the small *département* of Cantal (which has at least had the decency not to try to restore it or make a profit from it), but I will not let such administrative trivialities stand in my way. Of course, I know I cannot outrun my fate, only delay it a bit, but at least this final chapter of the story can be written partly on my own terms, if not on my own lands.

My departure from La Charlanne is beginning to take on the aspect of a permanent exile; there is no point in denying it. I concentrate on my preparations for leaving. From time to time I survey my immediate surroundings; I do not want to be caught off-guard again by the appearance of an enemy. My steps lead me eventually to the library.

I pack the books that I consider absolutely essential: the three volumes of *Fungi*, as well as *A se tordre: histoires chatnoiresques* by Alphonse Allais, and the indispensable *Voyages autour du monde et en Océanie par Bougainville, Cook, Lapérouse, Marion, Baudin, Freycinet, Duperrey, Dumont d'Urville*, revised and translated by M. Albert-Montémont and illustrated by Bocourt and Ch. Mettais (Paris, J. Bry the Elder, 1855), because it lends itself well to rereading, and to the little interruptions that always arise during a move. Neither do I forget to pack a supply of victuals, or *provisions de bouche*, as the adventure novels of the nineteenth century often put it.

Alas, one does not simply leave the place where one's destiny was sealed without some distress. I have just made a rather unsettling discovery. My mother must have cherished some literary aspirations. I found two vellum notebooks at the bottom of a hidden drawer I'd never known about, in the old cherrywood armoire in her bedroom—I know, I know, it's the old Gothic cliché of the secret manuscript, but I refuse to be held responsible if life imitates art, no matter how trite. The slightly erratic handwriting, coupled with the faded ink, confers a quasi-antique quality on the books that bears no relation to their actual age, since at least one of them is a journal spanning the years 1942-1955. The entries are infrequent and often trivial, though written with irreproachable literary panache. I note in passing that my sister's future caused her a great deal of worry, barely tempered by the pride she felt in my early successes in the Parisian legal sphere. Curiously, the diary mentions someone called Auguste, whose letters my mother seems to have awaited with rather suspicious eagerness. I have racked my brain, but the name *ne sonne aucune clochette*, it doesn't ring a bell. I don't remember anyone named Auguste. Is it a code name? Made up? Or a carefully concealed sweetheart? Could my mother have dared to take on the role of Emma Bovary in a dubious twentieth-century remake, only set amid the provincial mores of Limousin, right beneath my father's nose (buried in obscure mycological texts as it was)? And how was I to interpret the following quote, from the entry for January 18, 1948: "Cannot love be reduced to the simple and momentary need to be moved by an apparition which looks all the more perfect for all its strangeness? [Grøndhal, 1944]"? There is something quite *fishy* about it all, I'm sure you will agree.

It seems you can never truly know anyone in the end, even the people closest to you. The mystery will have to remain unsolved; I have neither the time nor the inclination to untangle it. But the incident has affected my concentration. How many secrets are taken to the grave every day; every year? The secrets of a passionate affair never discovered, or of the key to a disappearance, or a murder . . .

✳

Everything must disappear.

✳

I am planning a series of explosions, followed by a devastating fire. The laboratory, the barn, the château—all of it will have to be blown up, all the way to the Dordogne and perhaps beyond. To that end I am boning up on *The Anarchist Cookbook* in front of the fire, fine-tuning the last technical details.

Sleep, treacherously, evades me. I doze intermittently, sinking into dreadful nightmares. Men in white coats are chasing me through the Volvic-stone labyrinth; they are wearing long tunics, like a sort of tight-fitting djellaba, which fall well below the knee and should, logically, hold them back; keep them from running so fast. They look like monks in a trance. One of them carries a gold censer inlaid with diamonds, which sparkle so brightly that they blind me when I look back to see whether they're gaining on me. They chant my name—NI-KO-NOR, NI-KO-NOR—in sepulchral voices. The corridor is long, endlessly long. I stumble several times. I know that if they catch me, that will be the end, but the faster I run, the closer they get.

They are right at my heels now, and one of them has managed to grab hold of my velvet jacket. I manage to free myself with a jerk but there are more and more of them all the time; I am trapped in a giant termite mound, and I think one of them has an axe—a deeply tanned man who is gnashing his teeth and, I note fleetingly, bears an astonishing resemblance to Jack Nicholson in *The Shining*. The tunnel becomes wider and brighter, with a white, wintry, very artificial light. I shiver uncontrollably. The walls are covered with black and white photos that pass before my eyes—a series of alternating images of dead trees, and the faces of dead people. Stuck on an infernal moving walkway, I am doomed to look at them forever.

I wake with a start, exhausted and shaking. The grandfather clock in the drawing room strikes three.

I manage to fall asleep again. The setting has changed. Now I seem to be a guest at an enormous banquet in the great hall of an unknown château. Oversize crystal chandeliers shed a dazzling light on a table so long I can't see the end of it. Antique goblets sparkle in the glow. They are filled with a strange, bloody liquid. Artistically arranged platters of food are aligned in striking and exquisite crimson rows. I note as I draw closer that the dishes are unusual; as beautiful as jewels, but oddly unappetizing. Fly agaric caps covered with a fine, gleaming layer of quivering aspic nestle on an immense golden plate. Next to them I see a ramekin of large red berries. These are translucent like redcurrants but I do not recognize the species; perhaps they are the wolfberries I remember my mother talking about when I was a child? Pink-hued veal heads, laid out in a circle, occupy the place of honour.

The whole spectacle has a slightly macabre air of order and opulence—as well as a feeling of *déjà vu*, though I can't quite put my finger on what has inspired that. Large black flies dot the white tablecloth, as in some Renaissance still-life paintings. Bizarrely, they do not buzz away at my approach; they seem to be attached to the table, like some sort of lure. But I have other, more pressing concerns; the presence of the plate of fly agaric mushrooms is bothering me. Have they been boiled for a full ten minutes, in accordance with Doctor Pouchet's detoxification method? I have no way of telling. I make a mental note: do not touch the fly agarics, whatever happens.

The other guests are talking amongst themselves. They seem animated, and yet I hear their voices as if from far away; the snippets of conversation are like puzzle pieces put together by a deranged mind: "veal sweetbreads" — "misdemeanour" — "barely three minutes" — "taxidermist" — "mortified" — "the price of uncertainty" — "fits of laughter" — "silverware" . . . I have difficulty concentrating. Many of these people are perfect strangers to me.

But I am sure of one thing: there are men in white coats. Everywhere.

My parents are there, too.

I can see Antonin Berg at the head of the table, chatting to a man with a pointy nose. I think I recognize the tutor, Monsieur Feuillère. It's all very troubling. Waves of nausea wash over me. But no one seems to have noticed that I'm there. I note that the sounds are becoming clearer, as if I've finally found the right frequency. Grivaud, in a jovial mood, is regaling the company with salacious medico-legal anecdotes.

My father is explaining to the person next to him, with great seriousness, that the mushrooms on the large golden platter are not fly agarics, but rather sickener mushrooms ("or *Russula emetica*, a basidiomycete with an extremely bitter taste, my dear") studded with dots of white sugar—"An ingenious trick, don't you agree?" he says, winking, as he takes another large helping of breaded pigs' feet.

The master of ceremonies, a tall, willowy figure wearing a black leotard and a clown mask, prepares to give a toast. He raps the blade of his knife against a crystal wine glass, calling for silence, and then removes the mask with agonizing slowness.

Anastasie's face is revealed. She is very young, and very beautiful.

She turns her head to look at me silently, a cloyingly sweet look on her face. The other guests have stopped talking. The men in white coats have all stood up in a single movement and are making as if to come towards me.

I run. Now I am in a corridor so narrow that I can barely fit between its walls. After several seconds, minutes, light-years, I finally see a door, which I push open. The room is plunged into thick, viscous blackness; it's impossible to gauge its dimensions. I move forward cautiously, feeling my way by touch. I find another doorknob, which I turn guardedly. Another banquet table, identical to the first, is set out in the middle of an immense gallery, lit by pale, flickering candles. The table is empty except for a single golden platter, towards which I am irresistibly drawn.

Closer up, I can see that it is the same plate of fly agarics from the other banquet. I recognize it perfectly; there is no doubt about it. But one thing is not quite right.

The mushrooms are white with red spots.

This isn't possible. I rummage mentally through my store of mycological knowledge. *Amanita muscaria* is never coloured this way. It is always red with white spots; even the old texts attest to that. The great mycologists Antoine de Jussieu, Linnaeus, Paulet, Fries, and Saccardo must be spinning in their graves. I could even almost forgive Hadrianus Junius (de Jonghe) for that ridiculous business with *Phallus impudicus*, if it would give the fly agaric back its white spots!

I think I understand, finally. I am the victim of a mycological hoax. Some kind of good-natured ribbing, certainly. Inappropriate, yes, but just a simple joke! I nearly cry with relief. I can guess who is behind all of this. The important thing is not to react, because that is what she wants. I quickly regain my usual self-control.

There, I am almost calm again.

But then I see with alarm that the indelible, aberrant red spots of the ersatz fly agarics are beginning to spread across the backs of my hands, like a galloping case of smallpox. I scream, clasping my head in my hands. I am vaguely conscious of having become Munch's *The Scream*. Under the effect of the sound vibrations, the plate shatters into a million golden shards, like burning confetti, which fall on me before disintegrating with the smell of sulphur.

I am covered from head to toe with sticky fragments of fly agaric. The mutant pustules are still spreading across my skin.

It tastes like fear . . . I am on the edge of the abyss.

❋

I jerk awake again, this time for good. My linen sheets are drenched with sweat. I recover myself bit by bit, but the nausea and headache persist. Enough wild imaginings . . . what a horrendous scene, straight out of some Gothic novel . . . and yet I haven't consumed any hallucinogenic mushrooms, that I know of. But then where were all these fly agarics coming from? I hope this isn't an insidious return of the visions. Dawn is about to break at the château de la Charlanne. It is time to spring into action, to initiate the last phase of the plan. I must get dressed, have some breakfast, look one last time at the grapevine frieze in the kitchen.

This is not the time for weakness or indecision.

La Thébaïde will serve as my final refuge.

I really have nothing to complain about. That haven of *paix forestière* (*sylvestre*? *forestal*? The French language is singularly lacking in forest-related adjectives, regrettably; one must rely on the Scandinavian or Inuit language) is much more tranquil than the Florentine retreat of Fra Angelico, who was haunted by monstrous creatures there. The only monstrous company I receive will be of the metaphorical kind, my lifelong occasional companions.

I am ready to leave the château.

This morning I poured several containers of gasoline and other flammable liquids around the outbuildings (barn, shed, stable/laboratory), right up to the entrance to the property. I have also taken the time to burn any compromising papers and documents in a large copper cistern, though I couldn't bear to get rid of the photo albums. They will accompany me to La Thébaïde; I can decide later.

It tore at my heart to leave my mushroom maps. All my cep patches are listed there, with dates and analyses . . . it is a real loss for humanity. I should have been born in the era of the Academy of Lynxes; I should have been permitted to leave a mycological mark. I think I would have found satisfaction in that kind of destiny. But alas, I cannot take the risk of my *cartes à cèpes* falling into the wrong hands. There is too much at stake. I know that.

Then I went from room to room of the château, carefully soaking furniture, curtains, and carpets. Bedrooms, sitting rooms, kitchen, and even the library, proceeding with determination and efficiency. I gave each room a long look before leaving it, imprinting on my memory one last view of a world about to vanish.

I have no regrets. Everything has gone according to plan. I feel as if I'm carrying out a religious ritual, rather like a Tibetan monk about to immolate himself. Not everything will burn, of course; the stones, which have seen their fair share of fire, will undoubtedly survive the devastation—but that doesn't matter now.

We are only a few matches away from the final blaze, the *auto-da-fé*. The ultimate bonfire. The nearest fire station is twenty kilometres away; the closest neighbours two or three kilometres. By the time the alarm is raised and the inevitable, pathetic attempts at extinguishment begin, I will hopefully be safe at La Thébaïde.

The carbonized remains of the postman will perhaps be found in the DS. No matter. I will be far away. With a bit of luck, they might believe for a while that the corpse is mine, which would give me a greater head start over my pursuers. Before departing in the postal van, I go out to the cemetery one last time. I walk quietly down the hazel tree-lined path. Tender green leaves are just beginning to appear. The air is gentle; the world is at peace. I push open the creaky old metal gate and follow the tiny footpath, almost hidden beneath the grass. The tombstones have been overrun by the invasive presence of nature. The place has an air of abandonment, even more so than usual. I suppose there is a kind of balance in all of this; the ancient cemetery will be the perfect complement to the blackened ruins a hundred metres away. The whole scene will be rather romantic, reminiscent of Caspar Friedrich's *Abbaye dans une forêt de chênes* (1810). I wonder if the pine trees will infiltrate this place too. It's quite likely. But it will take two or three decades for nature to reassert itself, and for ceps to grow here. I will not be around to gather them. The thought of some unknown person hunting ceps in my domain perturbs me much more than it should. I pull myself together and, breathing deeply, pick my way towards my father's grave.

I was not meant to rest here.

The white marble headstone next to my father's is also covered by weeds; it is only with difficulty that a snippet of engraving can be seen: *Ana . . . 1922 — . . .*

Mon enfant, ma soeur, you did not want to die with me in the country that is so like you. Together, though, we could have conquered wild, vengeful parallel universes. Why did you do nothing with the sublime and scandalous destiny I offered you? Admit it; your treacherous gaze was always fixed on other horizons.

I cannot linger; it's too dangerous. I have to tear myself away from this place. I have never bothered much with nostalgia, and I am not about to begin now. Neither will I give in to sentimentality, a demonstration at least as despicable as irony; the two are Siamese twins, two sides of the same coin. But despite everything, I have to admit that I have a few butterflies in my stomach (or *papillons dans l'estomac*—another expression the French language would do well to adopt).

※

I know they are coming; they will be here soon. Perhaps they will all be dressed in white coats. It is difficult to be sure; the enemy, like a chameleon, can take on an endless array of disguises. But, ultimately, this will change nothing.

The outsiders are gathering . . . A new day is born.

Now that the path has been laid out, I feel a degree of peace and serenity.

I am taking the Clairefontaine notebook with me, obviously. If I ever have the misfortune to be captured alive (unlikely, but I shall leave nothing to chance), it is my life-insurance policy, my one-way ticket, the only document capable of presenting my defence in a clear and objective manner, of thoughtfully explaining my version of events. Of setting the record straight once and for all.

I will slip the notebook into a plastic sleeve and fasten it to my torso with strong adhesive tape. If they want it, let them come and get it. They will be signing their own death warrant.

Soon, because I must, because the die is cast, I will set off.

I will not return here. I cannot count on it. Is it my fault if life is nothing but fury and violence, and if the forests are doomed? There are no victims in this world, no persecutors; there are only possessed people in straitjackets. And when the shrieks of ancestral malediction echo throughout the Dordogne gorges to pursue and torture me, I will take refuge amidst the tranquillity of my inner landscape, where all is green, mossy, and timeless.

Despite everything, I might turn around just once, to see the château engulfed in flames. Or perhaps, as I sit at the wheel of my yellow car, I will look straight ahead of me, down the route des Ajustants, in search of a new sign.

A PARTIAL LIST OF SNUGGLY BOOKS

LÉON BLOY *The Tarantulas' Parlor and Other Unkind Tales*
S. HENRY BERTHOUD *Misanthropic Tales*
FÉLICIEN CHAMPSAUR *The Latin Orgy*
FÉLICIEN CHAMPSAUR *The Emerald Princess and Other Decadent Fantasies*
BRENDAN CONNELL *Clark*
QUENTIN S. CRISP *Blue on Blue*
LADY DILKE *The Outcast Spirit and Other Stories*
BERIT ELLINGSEN *Now We Can See the Moon*
EDMOND AND JULES DE GONCOURT *Manette Salomon*
RHYS HUGHES *Cloud Farming in Wales*
JUSTIN ISIS AND DANIEL CORRICK (editors) *Drowning In Beauty*
VICTOR JOLY *The Unknown Collaborator and Other Legendary Tales*
BERNARD LAZARE *The Mirror of Legends*
JEAN LORRAIN *Masks in the Tapestry*
JEAN LORRAIN *Nightmares of an Ether-Drinker*
JEAN LORRAIN *The Soul-Drinker and Other Decadent Fantasies*
ARTHUR MACHEN *Ornaments in Jade*
ARTHUR MACHEN *N*
CAMILLE MAUCLAIR *The Frail Soul and Other Stories*
CATULLE MENDÈS *Bluebirds*
LUIS DE MIRANDA *Who Killed the Poet?*
OCTAVE MIRBEAU *The Death of Balzac*
CHARLES MORICE *Babels, Balloons and Innocent Eyes*
DAMIAN MURPHY *Daughters of Apostasy*
KRISTINE ONG MUSLIM *Butterfly Dream*
YARROW PAISLEY *Mendicant City*
URSULA PFLUG *Down From*
JEAN RICHEPIN *The Bull-Man and the Grasshopper*
DAVID RIX *A Suite in Four Windows*
FREDERICK ROLFE *An Ossuary of the North Lagoon and Other Stories*
JASON ROLFE *An Archive of Human Nonsense*
BRIAN STABLEFORD *Spirits of the Vasty Deep*
TOADHOUSE *Gone Fishing with Samy Rosenstock*
JANE DE LA VAUDÈRE *The Demi-Sexes and The Androgynes*
RENÉE VIVIEN *Lilith's Legacy*

Printed in February 2023
by Rotomail Italia S.p.A., Vignate (MI) - Italy